International's Series in Economics

S

History and Structure
of
Economic Development

History and Structure
of
Economic Development

FRIEDRICH BAERWALD

Professor of Economics
Fordham University

INTERNATIONAL TEXTBOOK COMPANY
Scranton, Pennsylvania

Standard Book Number 7002 2230 8

73-2292

Copyright ©, 1969, by International Textbook Company

Library of Congress Catalog Card Number: 71-76406

Foreword

As the extended bibliography at the end of this volume testifies there has been a great outpouring of works, short and long, on the problems of economic development. This is the response of the professional economist to the challenge posed by the accelerating processes of population growth in economically retarded parts of the world, the spread of urbanization, and a radical restructuring of the labor force, particularly in advanced countries. There are many ways of analyzing these problems of economic development. Model building would be one, detailed studies of particular areas or countries another. The reason why the present volume is being offered to the public is that in many of the worthwhile publications little attention is paid to conditions and institutions of the economic structure as they have been shaped through historical processes. For instance, most volumes on the economy of Communist China start literally with the year 1949 when the Red Chinese had taken over the mainland. But to disregard the pull of historical forces of a country whose origins go back without basic loss of identity almost three thousand years is to impair our comprehension of the particular shape of problems arising in this setting of economic development. Equally, the longer view or historical perspective seems to be necessary in order to enable policy makers to choose models of development specifically fitted to these institutional and motivational configurations.

It is the purpose of this volume to extend the concept of economical development backward into history in order to make correct and effective forward projections of designs and programs for economic expansion and growth. A disregard of historically conditioned current situations has proved to be costly in early experiments of development aid and planning. Mathematical model building has brought considerable sophistication to the methods of programming economic development. To a certain extent data of historical relevance can also be put into computerized systems. But ultimately decisions dealing with economic development are not made in a laboratory setting. They are made by leaders who will not hand over the ultimate responsibility to specialized experts. Every concrete development process is therefore based on interaction between technicians and leadership groups. Economic analysis, understanding itself as analysis of social processes shaping the economic system and its sectors, must develop methods of comprehending total situations within which particular types of economic development occur or are either feasible or unrealistic. An attempt has been made to incorporate into this brief volume this point of view. Inevitably then the presentation has an interdisciplinary aspect combining such specialized endeavors as economic history, analysis of structures of development, and studies of comparative economic systems.

In this age of ever-increasing specialization in the social sciences and in economics perhaps an apology is in order for presenting a one-author volume on economic development. But while single authorship may have the disadvantage of a personal perspective, it has certain advantages in the analysis of policy problems and the design of programs. There must ultimately be a *unified* viewpoint, an overall comprehension of economic development in all its implications which alone can establish necessary and meaningful relations between various action programs and policies. The reader, it is hoped, will discover that in this book such a general conceptual scheme has been brought to the analysis of very diverse areas, patterns, and phases of development. Only in this perspective purely political and ideological assumptions and distortions about economic development can be reduced to the level of reality.

FRIEDRICH BAERWALD

New York, N.Y.
March 1969

Contents

chapter 1

Economic Development: History, Institutions, and Theory

As the year 2000 comes into view, problems of economic development assume increasing urgency. In the past, changes in population, technology, market structures, and social organization were spread out over long periods of time. For those living in such slower-paced eras, things seemed to be almost at a standstill. But beginning in the seventeenth century, the historical processes transforming economic and social institutions started to speed up.

In the year 1650 the world population numbered about 700 million. It had taken hundreds of thousands of years of prehistory and the six thousand years of recorded history to reach this figure. In 1840 the world population had grown to one billion; by 1930 it had doubled. Between that time and the present (circa 1970), it nearly doubled again. But in Latin America there has been a *tripling* of the population since 1920. In 1968 it is estimated that the world population was increasing by 190,000 people a day.

It may very well be that measures initiated to decelerate this trend in population growth will meet with some success in the next few decades. But this will not substantially relieve the pressures caused by regional imbalances between population and food production and by dangerous discrepancies between growing numbers of people on one side, and employment opportunities and educational facilities on the other. Congestion and deterioration of mushrooming urban areas are creating chronic crisis centers even in some advanced countries. This increases the strain on financial resources, especially of local governments.

These difficulties in economic and social development have multiplied even while technological progress maintains its momentum. Its potentialities are tremendous, especially in the peaceful use of atomic energy. Since

1967 a panel of experts from the Atomic Energy Commission, the Tennessee Valley Authority, various federal departments and universities have worked on a design for a nuclear-powered agro-industrial complex. Such projects could be located on the coast of arid land areas. Nuclear-energy power plants could be used to generate electricity and to desalt sea water. The desalinated water could then be used to irrigate huge tracts of arid land, to develop scientifically managed large-scale farms producing food for an estimated five million people while requiring only about 100,000 farm workers. The residual minerals gained in the desalting process could be used for a great variety of industrial purposes. In 1968 the Rockefeller and the Ford foundations announced joint grants to extend research in tropical agriculture, especially the development of rice and grain seeds adapted to hot and humid climates and of pastures and cattle breeds suitable for beef production in many parts of Latin America and Africa.

If economic development were merely an engineering problem or a matter of spreading advanced agricultural methods, the outlook would be bright. However, every economic system is part of a larger social system with its specific history, culture patterns, leadership and class structures, and all the conflicts and competitions characteristic of social relations. It is one thing to work out blueprints for optimum technical progress; it is quite another to translate such projects into economically and socially feasible policies of development. Actually problems of economic development cut across many disciplines of scholarly endeavor. They raise questions of government structure, educational levels, socially defined motivations and behavior systems, actual and potential resources and the all important problem of timing.

The availability of computers suggests strongly the working up of economic, social, and historical data into models representing the interrelation of these highly divergent factors so that guidelines for policies in specific development situations could be worked out with a great deal of confidence. Considerable work along these lines has been done in recent years.*

These decision models have improved the inventory of analytical tools; but they can never rule out the need to make prudential judgments about development policies in which historical intuition and political imagination must take a part. It is the purpose of this volume to outline typical historical perspectives which must be considered in the decision-making process regarding economic development. Furthermore, we will outline

*I. Adelman and E. Thorback (eds.) *The Theory and Design of Economic Development*, Baltimore, Md., Johns Hopkins Press, 1966.

basic concepts of development structures which must be used in order to make a correct identification of the actual situation to which development policies are to be applied. Recent experience in Southeast Asia has shown that purely quantitative, statistical approaches and mathematical representations of assumed factor interrelations are inadequate to deal with a total situation and that they can lead to serious errors in policy design and implementation.

In view of the urgency of the problems of economic development in the late twentieth century the margin for error becomes precariously narrow. A very consistent model for Maximum Speed Development (MSD) has been developed,* but to apply it as was suggested to Communist China constitutes a great error in judgment because this suggestion disregards the specific Chinese road to communism as frequently proclaimed by Mao Tse-tung. Before analytical models are to be applied, a thorough analysis must be carried out of the unique historical and social conditions underlying the developmental situation. If policies of development are based on a consistent but inapplicable model great disappointments are in store for policy makers and the intended beneficiaries.

The electronic age has brought about a revolution in the awareness of mankind. Instantaneous worldwide communications are breaking down barriers of distance and bringing undeveloped areas in touch with advanced regions. Technological advances in space, weaponry, agriculture, medicine, and industry have demonstrated to all the possibility of development and progress. Knowledge of these advances has reduced the old fatalistic acceptance of poverty and stressed the glaring discrepancies between the wealth of the few and the destitution of the many—precisely in those areas where population is still increasing rapidly while agricultural and industrial rates of growth remain relatively slow.

The speedy recovery and subsequent economic development in Europe and Japan after World War II cannot be understood unless we take into account the impact of historical conditions on managerial knowhow, work motivation, and administrative and technological abilities. But one of the most common fallacies in development policies, especially in their early days around 1950, was the assumption that the accumulated experience of the advanced Western countries has such general validity that it could be recommended and applied without serious modifications everywhere in the world.

*John C. H. Fei and Alpha C. Chiang, "Maximum Speed Development Through Austerity," in I. Adelman and E. Thorback (eds.) *The Theory and Design of Economic Development*, Baltimore, Md., Johns Hopkins Press, 1966.

Today it is generally understood that this assumption was a mistake. Yet this acknowledgment makes it even more necessary to study those long-run conditions shaping the social structure of countries in various phases of economic development in order to arrive at realistic and feasible methods and goals. For this reason we will link the study of basic patterns of economic history with the analysis of development models.

A BIRD'S-EYE VIEW OF ECONOMIC DEVELOPMENT

Economic development can be defined as a move toward ever more efficient and differentiated methods of supplying people with the requirements for survival and improvement. For hundreds of thousands of years man led an uncertain and precarious existence. Hunting and food gathering were the only alternatives to starvation and extinction. Suddenly between 10,000 and 5000 B.C. a series of "great leaps forward" were made. Man started to keep domestic animals and to plant crops. He learned how to produce pottery, to use hides and fibers for clothing, and to build boats. At the end of this period, village settlements had been established in Europe and irrigation systems were already in use in Mesopotamia and Egypt. Most important, writing was invented and clay tablets were the first material used to store and transmit information in the area of the Tigris and Euphrates Rivers.

These documents mark the transition from prehistory to recorded history. Economic development stretches far into the prehistorical period. The great inventions in agriculture and in the arts and crafts made in the 5,000 years prior to the onset of recorded history created a more dependable food supply, enabled people to *economize*—that is, to provide rationally not only for immediate needs but for later necessities and contingencies. The extension of the time horizon of economic activities beyond the immediate present made it possible for people to allocate more energy and time to the building up of differentiated forms of social organization.

By 2600 B.C. the economic and political structure of ancient Egypt based on the regular inundations of the Nile already presents an advanced and centralized system. At about the same time an urban system was developing in Mesopotamia, using elaborate irrigation techniques whose operation required efficient territorial management. In China, village culture in the Yellow River region was far advanced, with pottery, weaving, and copper metallurgy in wide use. Along the Indus River, village economies also flourished.

While in various parts of the world primitive stone-age village systems were superseded by more advanced structures about 5,000 years ago, stone-age culture has survived into the twentieth century in some isolated places, as in the interior of New Guinea. Primitive farming techniques continue in wide areas of India and Africa where the plow and the hoe were unknown. In Southern Mexico and in Malawi, Africa, land is still burned over prior to the planting of a crop—a destructive technique which in pre-Columbian America had proved so disastrous to the economy and political survival of the Maya Indians.

Here we encounter one of the great problems of economic development—the unevenness of its spread, the simultaneous existence of advanced and primitive systems. History discloses a fact that must be learned at the very start of any study of economic development: there has never been a sustained period of uninterrupted general economic progress. Around 100 A.D. the Roman economic system with its great achievements in urban development, road building, shipping, large-scale plantation agriculture, and efficient military and political organization seemed to be stable and destined for further growth and prosperity. Four hundred years later this economic system, after two centuries of gradual deterioration and erosion, had virtually disappeared. The economic system in the early Middle Ages was far more primitive and restricted in scope than that which flourished at the height of the Roman era.

The economic development of the Western world started, therefore, almost from zero around Roman cities which had become virtual ghost towns and in areas no longer connected by the efficient road system of the Roman period. Only gradually did the economy develop beyond the enforced self-sufficiency of huge manorial holdings through the rise of towns which were free of domination by territorial princes. There a social development occurred almost unique in the context of world economic history; the gradual rise of an independent middle class of artisans and merchants who owed their wealth to their economic efforts rather than to dependence on a basically political power structure. The discovery of the New World gave a tremendous impetus to trade through the production of such new cash crops as sugar, tobacco, coffee, and—somewhat later—cotton. The revival of the institution of slavery was a considerable source of profit for merchants from Northern Europe involved in this business. The new resources of gold and silver contributed toward the strengthening of the monetary structure. More funds became available for investment in large-scale enterprises. The revenues of government from excise taxes and tariffs also rose substantially.

The medieval economy already had evolved new rational and efficient business structures and methods such as the limited-liability company and double-entry bookkeeping. Now technology, or the systematic application of scientific methods to the art of production, was added to this evolving production and business system, and the foundations thus laid for an accelerated development of the Western economic system. In the relatively short period of 200 years this development led far beyond the levels achieved by either the Romans or the Chinese.

As industrialization and urbanization gained momentum, the economic system was for the first time subjected to scholarly analysis. Economics as a discipline arose simultaneously with the modern era which left all previous stages of economic achievement far behind. The main emphasis was on the exploration of market structures that would promise maximum levels of output and optimum conditions for the distribution of the national income. As was perhaps inevitable, from the very beginning economics operated with broad general assumptions about personal motivations and property, the nature of society, the structure of the market, and the role of government. A body of doctrines was formulated stressing the advantages of perfectly competitive markets and the self-regulating mechanisms of prices and profits. It found its classical expression in Adam Smith's *Wealth of Nations* which appeared in 1776.

Early in the nineteenth century and coeval with the growing pains of the factory system, contradictory doctrines about the nature and the social implications of the emerging industrial system were formulated. Ideological doctrines claiming to offer complete and perfect solutions for the achievement of maximum economic goals and optimum social conditions rivaled for attention and public support. Liberalism, offering a defense of the institutions of modern capitalism favored a private, individual profit-oriented market structure and maintained that perfect competition could adjust all short-term imbalances. Socialism was committed to public ownership of means of production and the replacement of private profit motivations by considerations of public needs. Economic development was viewed by Socialists as being propelled by the conflicting interests of capitalists and workers. The class-struggle concept was elevated to an exclusive method of historical and economic analysis. Political parties in Europe were identified with specific segments of people within the economic structure. Conservatives represented landowners and heavy industry, liberals spoke for the professional and commercial middle classes, socialists for workers. With the emergence of the Soviet Union after World

War I and of Communist China after World War II economic development seemed to be split into two utterly opposed systems each claiming superiority over the other.

But as modern technology spreads throughout the world, forcing scientific managerial procedures on production systems regardless of their legal form and of ownership relations, a process of demythologizing of economics has at long last gotten under way. What appeared even recently to be founded in basic differences in economic "philosophy" and social structure can now be more appropriately related to different points of departure in industrialization, different timing in processes of system transformation and to general cultural rather than specific economic differentiations. This does not mean that really essential differences on the level of general and of political philosophy have disappeared. But there is an unburdening of economic issues from overlays of ideologies.

Economic development is not merely a problem of emerging countries. It presents continuous challenges to already advanced economic systems. Because economic development occurs in a social setting which is at all times exposed to external pressures and internal strains and stresses, it would be shortsighted to think of it as ending up in a period of unchanging stability.

Economic development, because it is one aspect of history, is openended. In fact, one of the great fallacies of an ideological approach to economic problems and policies is to overlook this and to think in terms of end phases under such headings as capitalism or communism. While a consideration of economic development in a historical and social vacuum would be an exercise in futility, a purely descriptive or historical analysis would be equally unproductive. Theory construction, especially model building, is also required to enable us to assess more precisely the conditions that must prevail or must be created to promote and to sustain economic development. But for the purpose of this theoretical endeavor, it is necessary to use historical and social patterns of economic systems as building blocks. Abstract sector models of economic development have their uses, but they must be fleshed with insights that can come only from a consideration of historical patterns.

It is therefore the plan of this book to develop generalized concepts of historical structures of economic development, to bring into sharp focus basic contemporary problems of development—which will be called paradoxes—and to demonstrate their impact on comtemporary economic systems.

In order to relate this approach to the treatment of development in the writings of economists, it is advisable to outline the trends of thinking about these problems.

APPROACHES TO ECONOMIC DEVELOPMENT

The words "economic development" were introduced into economic theory shortly before World War I when Joseph Schumpeter published in German his *Theory of Economic Development.** Actually, this was a misleading title for a study that presented a somewhat novel contribution to business-cycle analysis. It will be instructive to dwell on this early twentieth-century effort by a renowned economist in order to throw light on the scope of the problems bearing on economic development.

Schumpeter (who shortly after publication of his book was appointed to Harvard University) was deeply rooted in the tradition of Austrian economics which, together with the work of such British economists as Stanley Jevons and Alfred Marshall, gained ascendancy over the original classical school of economics represented by Adam Smith, David Ricardo, and John Stuart Mill in the closing decades of the nineteenth century. Discarding the classical labor theory of value and the macrodynamic view of the economy, the neoclassical economists of the Austrian and British schools made a great advance in analysis by introducing the concept of marginal utility. But in doing so, they shifted from the macrosphere to an analysis of the microeconomic situation of individuals and of business firms. Of necessity there was a reduction of a long-run time framework of analysis to the short run. Actually, the theoretical model which was used by the neoclassical economists was of the stationary type, assuming given conditions of the size of the labor force, of capital, of productivity, and of consumer preferences. This meant that economic development as such was logically excluded from the analytical frame of reference—in sharp contrast to the longer and wider perspectives characteristic of the classical school.

For this reason Schumpeter's theory of economic development starts out with a brilliant analysis of the "circular flow" within a stationary economic system. This point of departure demonstrates his affiliation with economic neoclassicism. Like many other economists of this school (for instance the American, J. B. Clark[†]), Schumpeter viewed business fluctua-

*See the English translation published by Oxford University Press, 1935.
[†]J. B. Clark, *Distribution of Wealth*, New York, Macmillan, 1902.

tions as temporary departures from a stationary equilibrium position of the economic system. It was assumed that business cycles were temporary disturbances of this static state encompassing plus and minus deviations from a long-run condition of basically unchanging stability. Schumpeter emphasized the temporarily unstabilizing intrusion of entrepreneurs. These innovators had the imagination, according to Schumpeter, to devise new combinations of business, to stimulate investment and thereby generate a general upward trend in economic activities. This upswing was reinforced by some sort of bandwagon psychology, thus pushing the total level of transactions to greater heights. Since according to Schumpeter all this happened within a framework of oscillation around a stationary equilibrium, the forward momentum of the economy could not go on forever. It was inevitably followed by a reversal of upward trends. Now the upswing phase of the cycle brought about by the periodic and mysteriously ever-recurrent appearance of entrepreneurs is what is called *economic development* by Schumpeter. It should be clear, however, that this was a misnomer. The theory did not deal with economic growth. Schumpeter explicitly rejected any consideration of "exogenous" factors from his analysis. He specifically prescinded a consideration of the impact of changes in population and in technology. Only internal, purely economic magnitudes were considered in Schumpeter's analysis of so-called economic development. But such a narrowing down of the view makes a study of economic development virtually impossible. Actually, the classical school provides a far more valid approach to the problem. Contemporary efforts to formulate theories and policies of economic development must be based on this earlier approach and move forward from there. We will therefore examine more closely the classical understanding of economic development as it has been summarized by John Stuart Mill.*

The main body of Mill's *Principles of Political Economy* deals with problems of production, employment for labor, accumulation of capital, and the so-called population law which he took over from Thomas Malthus. Throughout the treatment of these topics Mill employs a long-run analysis. He assumed that expansion of production would eventually lead to an ever-increasing cost of output or, what is its reverse, diminishing returns. According to him, input-output ratios were doomed to become more and more unfavorable with additional inputs yielding ever-declining additional increments of output. For this reason he also believed that the rate of profit was bound to approach zero in the long run. Strangely

*J. S. Mill, *Principles of Political Economy*, 1848. The quotations in this section are from the second edition (Modern Library, Inc., New York).

enough, Mill considered the sections of his *Principles* dealing with these trends in production and profits as presenting "The economic laws of a stationary and unchanging society." Actually, doctrines emphasizing the law of diminishing returns and the tendency of the rate of profit to fall are theories of economic development of a specific type. They imply that there are built-in limitations to economic growth and development; that starting from a given point the rate of growth is bound to decrease, and that ultimately there will emerge a stationary state. This in fact was the view of John Stuart Mill. In Book IV of the *Principles* he speaks of "This impossibility of ultimately avoiding the stationary state—this irresistible necessity that the stream of human industry should finally spread itself out into an apparently stagnant sea. . . ." However far from deploring this assumed inevitability of stagnation, Mill disagrees with the "political economists of the old school" who viewed tendencies toward stagnation with alarm. He actually asserted that a stationary state "would be, on the whole, a very considerable improvement on our present condition." Actually, the reasons that he offers for this preference are philosophic rather than economic. Furthermore, Mill himself listed a number of reasons why for a considerable period of time the actual state of the economy will be dynamic—or, as he often calls it, "progressive." It is this aspect of Mill's *Principles* which are most instructive for a study of the framework of economic development even in this late stage of the twentieth century.

In discussing the progressive state of the economy, Mill intends to add a theory of motion to the theory of equilibrium which he, like most other nineteenth-century economists, incorrectly identified with a stationary state. In his outline of the dynamics of the political economy he stresses in the main three points:

1. The unlimited growth of man's power over nature.
2. The increase of the security of person and property.
3. An improvement in the business capacities of the general mass of mankind.

Before undertaking a more detailed study of these three points and their relation to problems of economic development and historical factors in economic growth, we should note that, from the viewpoint of neoclassical economics and of the theories of development directly or remotely derived from them, the rather sweeping statements of Mill seem to be irrelevant. Nevertheless, they serve their purpose in placing economic development in a wider historical and social setting. They are particularly useful if read against the experience accumulated in over a hundred years of actual progress. We of the late twentieth century are much better equipped than Mill of the nineteenth to realize that there is always another side to progress achieved, that the solution of problems of production creates new difficulties, so that Mill's "progress of civilized society" is rather ambiguous in nature.

Although Mill looked forward to a vast multiplication and long succession of inventions and, as we have seen, spoke of the unlimited growth of man's power over nature, he could not possibly have forseen the acceleration in technological advances that characterizes the twentieth century. He was indeed highly optimistic about the effects of rising technical standards and physical volumes of production. While in his chapters on wages he adhered to the erroneous wage-fund theory promising only continued subsistence levels of existence to the working class, in his chapter on the progressive state he correctly visualized that not only might the rich grow richer but many of the poor might also grow rich, and "the intermediate classes might become more numerous and powerful and the means of enjoyable existence be more and more largely diffused."

This sanguine interpretation of technical progress implies that economic development brought about by greater control of natural resources, far from creating unemployment, would increase job opportunities and raise the income of workers. Unlike David Ricardo* and Karl Marx, Mill did not carry his analysis to the point where technological unemployment would emerge. Like most nineteenth-century economists, Mill did not include agriculture in his consideration of economic development and progress. From the viewpoint of the late twentieth century, however, it has become clear that in the United States, the most advanced industrialized country in the world, the productivity of agriculture has risen at an even faster rate than that of industry, and it is precisely in the farm sector that technological labor displacement has taken place on a large scale. This aspect of technological progress becomes clearly visible in advanced as well as as in emerging countries. It exercises increasing pressure on the facilities and financial resources of local government because more and more the rural masses move to urban centers to extricate themselves from unemployment or underemployment.

There is another aspect of the increasing control of man over nature which was not and perhaps could not be foreseen by Mill in the nineteenth century. While technological progress has vastly diminished distances between various parts of the world and has created instantaneous worldwide

*David Ricardo, *The Principles of Political Economy and Taxation,* Chapter XXXI on Machinery (Modern Library, Inc., New York).

communication, the great acceleration in the growth of old and new industries in advanced countries has actually widened the gap between highly developed and underdeveloped areas. That is not to say that certain former colonial areas had not made substantial progress while under control of European nations in the period ending shortly after World War II.

This limited sharing in the fruits of economic development of advanced countries was just sufficient to bring many native populations to the awareness of their dependency and to the awakening of a strong desire to gain independence. But virtually everywhere this social and economic advance had not reached a stage where native leadership groups, managers, engineers, and administrators were available in adequate numbers to assure a stepping up or even a continuation of economic development at the previous rate once a status of political independence had been obtained. This retrospective view of Mill's concepts of economic development makes clear that for any understanding of the structure and the problems of development it is absolutely essential to define very carefully the historical point of departure and to include a systematized assessment of the present impact of past social structures into the design of schemes for further advance of the system.

The unevenness of technological development can also be viewed as causing a wide gap between formal political and economic structures and actual social change. The latter often move ahead much slower than the former. For this reason the second point made by Mill in his enumeration of factors conducive to economic development also appears quite different in our present postcolonial period from what it looked like to a nineteenth-century observer living in the British Empire. This point referred, as we have seen above, to the increase of the security of person and property. The short period of national socialism in Central Europe and the first four decades of communism have shown only too painfully that there is no necessary or inevitable relation between economic progress and the security of person and property. On the other hand, it must be conceded that the breakup of external order as it prevailed in many former colonies and the rising insecurity in many areas caused by tribal rivalries together with the ineffectiveness of central governments have placed a firm break on the momentum of economic development precisely in those areas of economic growth that need acceleration rather than a slowdown.

The third point of Mill's concept of economic development—the improvement in the business capacity of people—is also far more ambiguous today than it may have appeared in the nineteenth century. In many parts of the world—for instance in Russia and in Southern Europe—illiteracy was widespread at the time Mill formulated his doctrines. Since that time, elementary education has made enormous strides almost everywhere and literacy has spread at a fast rate—although in areas where population is increasing very rapidly (as in most Latin American countries) the expansion of education facilities has not kept pace with the even faster rise of the numbers of young people, thereby keeping illiteracy ratios high despite all efforts to build schools and train teachers.

In some advanced countries, especially in the United States, the great emphasis on school attendance at least until the completion of the sixteenth year has not prevented a state of functional illiteracy from prevailing in some sections of the labor force. Obviously, this has not curtailed rapid economic development in the United States. But it has, at the same time, led to the exclusion of large numbers of people who are considered deficient in educational standards from sharing fully in the advantages of a progressive and abundant system. So again we encounter the fact that Mill's concepts of the prerequisites for economic development are as a two-edged sword that cuts both ways. Here we see again that the three-point scheme of Mill has considerable relevance for the understanding of the structure of economic development. While it is true that these elements of the social environment in which economic development must take place cannot easily be expressed in a quantitative manner, it would be a mistake to disregard them merely for this reason. Actually, they have great bearing on the way in which such factors in economic development as labor, capital, and management function. They must be considered in the formulation of reasonable expectations concerning the timing and the results of economic development.

As we continue to reappraise Mill's nineteenth-century concepts of economic progress we find one last area in which his expectations and those of his contemporaries did not come true. It is important to dwell on it because the actual course of history has created new and serious problems of economic development which could not be foreseen a century ago. There was a widespread conviction in the middle of the past century that at long last the period of great wars, such as the Thirty Years' War, the War of the Spanish Succession, the Seven Years' War, the French Revolutionary, and Napoleonic wars had come to an end. Actually, the three wars which occurred under Prussia's "Iron Chancellor" Bismarck in the period 1864-71 were of extremely short duration as compared to these older conflicts and world wars and recent conflicts of the twentieth century. It will be enlightening to read rather carefully what Mill had to say on this subject in his chapter on the Progressive State:

> Wars and the destruction they cause, are now usually confined, in almost
> every country, to those distant and outlying possessions at which it comes
> into contact with savages.

Some years before the first (1848) edition of Mill's *Principles*, British naval power had compelled the Chinese empire to open up the area of Canton to merchants including those dealing in opium, the use of which had been outlawed in China. Let us assume, however, that Mill did not really include the Chinese in his reference to "savages." More likely he was thinking of Africa. At any rate, his view of "distant and outlying possessions" shows a narrowing down of a worldwide perspective to a position in which other continents and their inhabitants were viewed as mere appendages to northwestern European—primarily British—political, military, and commercial power. Economic progress, then, was viewed as a projection of these interests and structures to the rest of the world. Natives were expected to become beneficiaries of this development to a certain extent, but were supposed to remain passive recipients of these advantages—not to become partners in the building up of the resources, business, and administrative institutions.

After World War I this one-sided, domination-submission relationship between advanced countries and colonial areas came under increasing pressures. However, the pattern survived until the end of World War II when, spurned on by the United States, the decolonization process began and was virtually completed twenty years later. This change—for which totally insufficient preparations had been made—altered the political aspects of the situation far more rapidly than the underlying economic conditions. Even today progress in formerly colonial areas is not possible without cooperation and assistance from advanced countries such as the United States, West Germany, and most of the former colonial powers. But the emphasis is now on aiding these newly independent countries to take over more and more responsibility for the design and the carrying out of measures leading them to higher levels of output, diversification of production, industrialization, and general upward movement of the world's economy.

This change in the world situation had led to a more differentiated approach to the conceptualization of economic development in terms of theory and model formulation. First of all, economic development is now viewed by most writers and experts in this field as strictly a problem of emerging nations. It is no longer viewed as an extension to a worldwide scale of economic progress in Northwestern Europe and the United States. This leaves outside of current development theory the very serious problems of advanced economies to maintain a balanced forward momentum in times of peace. Secondly, development models set up for comparatively primitive areas whether emanating in East or West assume that in one way or another these developing countries will imitate methods and social techniques identified with these advanced systems.

One way to conceptualize economic development in emerging countries is to distinguish between a "subsistence sector" and the "capitalist sector." W. Arthur Lewis in his analysis, "Economic Development with Unlimited Supplies of Labor,"* defines the capitalist sector as "that part of the economy which uses reproducible capital and pays capitalists for the use thereof." While the distinction between the subsistence and the capitalist sector is helpful for purposes of analyzing the changing relations between traditional and modernizing parts of a developing economy, the use of the word "capitalist" for the latter is too narrow for a general theory of development. Experience has shown that in many developing countries capital is being created not by entrepreneurs but in the form of public or at least publicly controlled enterprises. The inadequacy of Schumpeterian model of economic development as applied to countries which still have a large subsistence sector is clearly evident in Lewis' treatment of the role of savings and investment in such an economic setting. According to him, the central problem is to understand under what circumstances a customary rate of saving and investing 4 or 5 percent of the national income can be increased to about 12 or 15 percent. The main argument of Lewis is that this will be possible only through a prior increase in profit. While this proposition is entirely logical within the framework of the capitalistic model of economic development, it is too narrow to permit application in most cases of actual economic development. Actually, the more general term covering both capitalistic and noncapitalistic structures of economic development is *surplus*. Let us now turn to other concepts of contemporary development theory which will prove to be more helpful.

In his *The Strategy of Economic Development*† Albert O. Hirschman views the problem of investment in the same way we have presented it in the preceding paragraph. Only in advanced countries in which most economic activities are centered in the private sector, does the main proportion of investments come from savings. It must be added, however, that in highly industrialized countries in which large corporations account for the greatest proportion of output, these savings arise predominantly in the

*Reprinted in B. Okun and R. W. Richardson, *Studies in Economic Development,* New York, Holt, 1961.
†New Haven, Conn., Yale University Press, 1963.

business sector; they are only to a very limited extent emanating in individual households. In advanced countries a great deal of growth is financed through prices charged by corporations to individuals and to government. They are being set at a level which assures revenues high enough to accumulate internal funds for expansion.

With regard to underdeveloped countries the relation between savings and investment is entirely different. In many cases original capital investment comes from the outside. In the colonial period and throughout the nineteenth century a great deal of private capital flowed from Europe to the Western Hemisphere and elsewhere. It helped to finance railroads and public utilities as well as some industries. In fact, throughout this period European investors very often neglected investment opportunities at home, preferring the higher returns from foreign investment.

Private foreign investment is still a significant factor, but it must be noted that after World War II it has gone to a large extent from the most advanced country, the United States, to other highly developed areas such as Western Europe. While this has been very helpful to these countries and has enabled them to reach unprecedented levels of prosperity, this type of private capital outflow has not made a contribution to the narrowing of the gap between advanced and developing countries. This area has been left to public activities both in the form of new international financial institutions and of foreign-aid programs of advanced countries financed out of general taxation. Before we inspect the scope of these activities in the next section, it is necessary to set up some basic concepts.

A valid distinction is being made by Hirschman and others between social overhead capital (SOC) and direct production assistance (DPA). One of the decisive differences between the industrial development in Western countries and in currently emerging nations is the fact that industrialization in the West was preceded by centuries of a gradual build-up of resources. The seventeenth century saw the beginning of extensive road and canal building; there was a substantial increase in the number of professionally trained people in law, finance, and administration; city governments had reached high standards of municipal administration. Hence a considerable amount of SOC was already in existence when modern industry started its spectacular growth. The basic requirements for the operation of an *infrastructure* had already been met. To rush into industrialization without a prior build-up of such structures, especially an extension of basic educational and health facilities in formerly underdeveloped countries, would merely accentuate the imbalance of the overall situation and would in all likelihood fail to achieve output goals. It follows that in such development situations careful planning is required to find the proper mix between SOC and DPA aspects of investment in developing countries.

Whereas during and after World Was I political leaders were clinging to the illusion that defeated nations would somehow be able to pay monetary reparations to the victorious allies, the failure of these schemes which became final during the Great Depression of the 1930's convinced the authorities during World War II that there should be no new interallied debt resulting from military and economic assistance and that in the post-war period the main concern should be on economic reconstruction rather than on reparation. The period after World War II saw the inauguration of vast programs of economic aid. Before we describe the various agencies involved, it is necessary to make some basic distinctions in the matter of development assistance.

For all practical purposes the Marshall Plan of 1947 provided assistance to temporarily weakened but basically highly developed countries in Western Europe. Early in 1949 President Truman first outlined a system of technical assistance to developing countries. Once countries in Western Europe and the Soviet Union had entered into a new era of economic expansion, they also began to extend economic aid.

Basically economic aid has been given in the past twenty-five years in two entirely different settings. The first type of aid, exemplified by the Marshall Plan, can be classified as *reconstruction assistance.* This was designed as a short-range program; its application to already developed countries proved to be successful beyond all expectations at the time of its inauguration. This type of foreign assistance has long ceased, and most countries having received loans in connection with the plan have repaid their financial obligations to the United States. Aid to emerging nations falls under the category of *development assistance.* It is particularly necessary in countries exposed to population pressures while their resources and nonagricultural sectors are unable to deal with this imbalance. On the other hand, there are also development patterns in which comparatively little reliance is being placed either on reconstruction assistance or development aid. While they are not completely excluded, the main emphasis in this *bootstrap* model is on accumulation of capital through imposed austerity, especially restraints on consumption. Sometimes this is connected with tax incentives for priority investment. This has been used, for instance, in Puerto Rico and, as we will see, with notable success in West Germany.

AGENCIES FOR ECONOMIC DEVELOPMENT

We have already seen in the preceding section that economic development requires the awakening and the improvement of energies and resources without which a successful start to higher levels cannot be made. There must be a considerable extension of social overhead capital in terms of basic improvements of the productive, educational and social structures of emerging countries.

The United Nations has set up a number of agencies which are operating in this area. It would be quite wrong to dismiss these agencies as mere debating societies or sounding boards. Their very existence demonstrates the growing awareness of and a continuous and systematic concern for the various aspects of economic development.

The Food and Agricultural Organization (FAO) is concerned not only with improvements in agricultural production, but also with nutrition and living standards. The information accumulated in the work of this organization is an important tool in the design of assistance programs and domestic plans for development. This agency has its headquarters in Rome, Italy. The United Nations Educational, Scientific and Cultural Organization (UNESCO) is located in Paris. While some of its objectives are in the general field of human rights and freedom, it also has established programs for the reduction of illiteracy and has sponsored activities to spread educational skills through adult education.

The World Health Organization (WHO) located in Geneva has as its primary objective the raising of health standards throughout the world. It has become very widely known to travelers through the International Health Passports in which vaccination records are to be entered. There is no doubt that its activities have contributed to improving health standards, as evidenced by declining infant mortality rates and the notable absence of epidemics even in cases of large-scale dislocations of populations as a result of war or political upheavals.

The United Nations Children's Fund (UNICEF) is also of significance for economic development because it collects and distributes funds from governments and individuals to assist developing countries in improving child-care services.

We have listed only those agencies of the United Nations that have been assigned specialized functions in specific areas of economic development. Before we turn to international financial agencies connected with problems of development, it is advisable to outline briefly the operation of the Economic and Social Council of the United Nations. This assembly usually meets twice a year and affords an opportunity to the member states to discuss broad issues of policy which are considered not strictly political in nature. The latter problems are left to the general assembly of the United Nations. The Economic and Social Council is concerned with international economic, social, and cultural affairs and in this sense can supply guidelines to the operating agencies which have been mentioned earlier in this section; To facilitate the work of the Council, regional economic commissions have been set up for Europe, Asia, and the Far East, for Latin America and for Africa. While it is inevitable that politics and great-power rivalries enter the discussions, there is nevertheless considerable value to the proceedings of the Council and its regional commissions.

Many agencies are operating in the vital field of international finance. We will confine our discussion to those which are involved in economic development. The most important institution is the International Bank for Reconstruction and Development (World Bank) whose specific purpose is to provide financial facilities for development projects. One of its main functions consists in raising funds for the financing of specific development projects or to provide loans for such purposes. It should be noted that the activities of the World Bank are centered on direct production assistance (DPA), but a good deal of the loans can also be classified as supporting the enlargement of social overhead capital. Closely associated with the World Bank are two other agencies which are active in economic development, the International Development Association (IDA) and the International Finance Corporation (IFC).

The World Bank, very often in conjunction with the other two international financial agencies mentioned here, is also making available funds to the vital agricultural sector in developing countries. To illustrate: in the annual report 1965-66 loans for irrigation schemes in the amount of $45 million were made available in Malaysia; Mexico received $19 million for the same purpose. Paraguay received credits for the improvement of livestock production. Much larger amounts of loans are involved in the financing of industry. India received a credit of $100 million to enable Indian enterprises engaged in the production of commercial vehicles, machine tools, and electrical equipment to purchase additional tools to expand their output.

By far the greatest part of activities of the World Bank has been dedicated to the financing of social overhead capital, especially development of electric power and transportation. Funds were also made available for the improvement of water supply. The activities of the World Bank and the financial agencies connected with it have also reached into the field of education in developing countries. This was done in order to assist emerging nations to staff their infrastructure with skilled native personnel. For instance, during the year 1965-66 Chile, Ethiopia, Morocco, and Pakistan have received a total amount of almost $34 million to enlarge their educational facilities. We will now show the overall activities of the World Bank by summarizing from the report for 1965-66 the loans given for the various purposes of economic development.

Bank Loans and IDA Credits by Purpose, 1965-66
(Millions of U.S. dollars)

Transportation	$384.05
Electric power	254.50
Industry	232.50
Telecommunications	41.80
Agriculture	152.40
Education	33.95
Water supply	22.40
Engineering study	1.70

This table shows clearly that the greater part of the loans and credits are going into transportation and electric power development. It should be noted that among the recipients of these funds are not only emerging nations. Such well developed countries as Finland and Japan received $1.20 million and $1.25 million respectively for road building. However, the bulk of the funds did go to emerging and underdeveloped countries.

In addition to the loans and credits made available by the World Bank and the IDA, the IFC has made very substantial investment, standby and underwriting commitments especially to Latin American countries. In the period 1956-66 this corporation negotiated 124 commitments with a total value of $172.4 million. In addition to the financial activities of these international banks and corporations a great deal of economic aid is being given every year by advanced countries to developing nations. While the United States was first in extending this assistance, it was joined in this type of activity by the European Common Market, the Soviet Union, and other states of the Soviet bloc, and even to a small extent by Red China. Israel is extending technical assistance to a number of new nations in Africa. In the fiscal year 1967 the United States allocated $1,915 billion for nonmilitary grants and credits. By far the largest proportion of these funds were allocated to Asia. India and Pakistan received the largest individual amounts of economic aid, if we prescind the almost half-billion dollars that went to South Vietnam under this title. South Vietnam alone received more than double the economic aid appropriation for all of the Western Hemisphere.

The effectiveness of development assistance programs depends to a large extent on the standards and motivations prevailing in the ruling groups and administration of recipient countries. In many parts of the Far and Near East distinctions between public and private funds, between the public interest and the interest of one's own family have traditionally been far more blurred than in the Western world, where—deriving from the Roman concept of the *fiscus*—public and private assets have been traditionally separate. In China the imperial appointees in the provinces had to raise the cost of their own administrative budgets from revenue collections carried out under their jurisdiction. It is easy to see, then, that when development assistance is given, especially in the highly questionable form of budget support there are great leakages and far less than the scheduled total expenditures reach the actual development projects. Even where administrative standards come much closer to standard European and American concepts such as in Latin America, development aid may be hampered by the rigidity of the social structure.

It is for this reason that the "Alliance for Progress" between the United States and Latin American countries has stressed the interrelation between development assistance and social reform, especially in redistribution of land. We will see in the next chapter that some beginnings have been made in Latin American countries in this respect. Nevertheless in many developing countries in which there exist, as a carryover from feudalism and colonialism, extreme disparities between the wealth of the few and the poverty of rural and urban masses, rational use of aid and the design of development goals are often impeded by traditions of monumentalism—emphasis on prestige public construction, industrial installations, on national airlines, and on too much unregulated import of expensive consumer goods. This situation has created inbalances in development. Improvements in the subsistence sector are too slow to meet population pressures. Actually, the use of general budgetary aid in the assistance model which was practiced for a considerable period of time is bound to have these unsatisfactory results. The development assistance model is far better served by aid in DPA projects of a specific type.

The preceding discussion has shown that narrowly technical approaches to economic development overlooking the impact of long-established social and political patterns are bound to lead to serious errors in the formulation and carrying out of development policies. A discussion of economic development must be informed by certain insights into economic history. Judgments concerning the feasibility of development programs must take the historical context into account. They must be made with full knowledge that economic history is economic development seen retrospectively, and that economic development is, in effect, economic history in the making.

Attempts have been made recently to employ econometric methods in which some of the factors of government structure, procedures, and leadership motivations have been brought into the data universe. It is doubtful, however, that these models have great significance in the actual working up of designs for developmental goals. One of the great difficulties is that these factors are eminently qualitative and historically differentiated. For this reason development theory and policy must be informed more broadly by an understanding of economic history and of the problems of its interpretation.

APPROACHES TO ECONOMIC HISTORY

In the nineteenth century the historian Leopold von Ranke stated that it is the task of the historical scholar to find out "what really happened." The main research technique he recommended was a critical and complete study of documents in order to reconstruct as correctly as possible the course of events. From the very beginning of a concern with economic as distinct from political history which also developed in the last century, it was clear that the emphasis in economic history would have to be different. What was at stake was not a sequence of events and their ramifications, but a study of the patterns and changes of economic institutions and behavior over longer periods of time. A study of economic history in any other way presents great difficulties. In the culture system of the Greeks, Romans, and Chinese economic activities including trade and commerce, while considered indispensable, were nevertheless looked down upon as not really worthy of being recorded in historical treatises. Hence, to find out what the actual scope of economic activities was, it is necessary to resort to an examination of business records, of legislation, of occasional references in literature, and other widely scattered evidence. While this type of research is going on and is continuously producing new information, it must be realized that not everything that ever happened becomes thereby an historical fact. History as commonly understood is that part of the past which had significance above and beyond the instant of time in which an event occurred. It refers to those elements of development which made for continuity and change, for transformation and growth. That this has been the operational concept at least of economic history is clear from the evidence of the "phases and stages approach." We will turn our attention to it because these concepts have a great bearing on our understanding of economic development.

The "phases and stages"* approach to economic history—regardless of differences between the various authors—have in common the idea that every later stage is more advanced than the preceding one, and that there is a phase in which the economy is fully developed and will cease to undergo further transformations. Friedrich List[†] mentions five stages of development ranging from savage to a final agricultural, manufacturing, and commercial stage. One of the main points in List's approach to economic development was the assertion that no nation wants to be frozen into a less developed condition at a time when others have reached already a more advanced phase. Because of Britain's commanding lead in industry in the early nineteenth century, he opposed free trade on the grounds that it would force a large number of countries to remain predominantly agricultural and prevent them from reaching the manufacturing stage. For this reason List, who for a time worked together with the American economist Henry Carey, advocated protective tariffs in order to enable infant industries in agricultural countries to get started and eventually become competitive with European industries which already had been in existence for longer periods of time. It is, however, not correct to portray List as an archprotectionist. List always viewed economic problems in a long-run perspective. For him, the difference between macroeconomic and microeconomic analysis was precisely in the time framework of reference. He pointed out that such problems as resource preservation and development cannot be handled in the private sector, that they require long-range targets beyond the scope of individual small-scale enterprise. But while List demanded protection of domestic industries, he insisted on free competition within a country. Far from advocating protection as a device to enable industries in certain countries to continue forever operating at a high cost level, he stressed the significance of competition to force upon management ever increasing efficiency so that the price difference between foreign and domestic products eventually could be eliminated. Protection was acceptable only as a transitional policy in a period of incipient industrialization. Like John Stuart Mill he overrated an innovation of his own time, the electric telegraph. Pointing out that governments could now communicate much faster than in the age of the stagecoach, he expressed

---

*See B. F. Hoselitz, "Theories of Stages of Economic Growth" in his *Theories of Economic Growth*, New York, Free Press, 1960.

[†]Friedrich List *The National System of Political Economy*, New York, A. M. Kelly, 1966.

the hope, tragically refuted by subsequent history, that the telegraph would lead to world peace. Having been the chief architect of the lifting of internal tariff frontiers in the area of the German Confederation (1815-1866), he clearly foresaw in his essay on world peace the European Common Market which became a reality more than a hundred years later.

List's basic concept of economic development—namely, that it cannot be confined to certain privileged areas but is bound to become worldwide in scope—is a lasting contribution to the understanding of problems of economic development. The nineteenth century produced many other historical approaches to economics. One representative of the historical school, Bruno Hildebrand, shied away from the type of generalization implied in the scheme of List. He pointed out that political organization and cultural patterns may influence the evolution of the various successive stages of economic development. The implication here is clearly that different types of culture would set different economic goals. While political structure and culture are, as we already have stressed in this chapter, aspects of the total situation that cannot be overlooked in any analysis or design of economic development, Hildebrand's concept would ultimately lead to a situation in which underdeveloped countries would forever stay that way. Hildebrand denied the inevitability of a universal achievement of the most progressive stage of economic development, and he developed an economic phase concept of his own. According to him, the original state of the economy was distribution through barter. This was followed by a general spread of a monetary system. In turn, the money economy was to be superseded by a credit economy. While credit has a great role in economic development, it is at best merely an extension of the money system from a cash to a bookkeeping arrangement. It is superior to the cash-and-carry economy of the old days, but monetary facilities in themselves cannot generate economic development which must be carried out on the real level of output and technical progress.

Another well-known approach to economic history was undertaken by Karl Buecher.* He identified three stages of economic development in Western and Central Europe: the phase of a closed domestic economy in which manorial estates are self-sufficient, producing everything they require from food to simple consumer goods; the phase of the city economy in which there is production for a local market and a direct exchange between producer and customer; the stage of the national economy in which there is production for a larger market through the intermediary of

---

*Translated into English under the title *Industrial Evolution,* New York, 1901. (This title is a rather inadequate translation of *Die Entstehung der Volkswirtschaft.*)

merchants. These three phases are better understood as models or ideal types. In the earlier decades of the Middle Ages when the manorial estates predominated, merchants were active on an international level. Nevertheless, the large bulk of all goods produced emanated from the domestic economy. Merchants played an ever-increasing role in the later Middle Ages, and in many instances acquired great wealth. The transition to a national economy, however, occurred when roads became better and more secure, when transportation was speeded up on canals and rivers and when the whole system of distribution became more differentiated through the emergence of wholesalers and the establishment of the first factories.

There is no denying the fact that many underdeveloped countries today still fall under his first phase, the domestic economy in their subsistence sector. It does not necessarily follow that they must go first through the second phase before achieving the third one. Actually, when Buecher wrote his essays on economic development toward the end of the nineteenth century there was in existence an international economy of a vast scale. Between the end of the Napoleonic Wars and the World War I there occured a huge outflow of capital from Europe to North and South America and to other parts of the world. International transactions increased very rapidly. Advanced countries such as England, Germany, and France became more interested in the expansion of export industry and trade than in the development of internal mass consumption markets.

The concepts of the various phases and stages of economic development which we have discussed so far represent a progressive unfolding of economic structures from simple to more differentiated systems. They do not go to any great extent into the interrelations between various levels and types of economic organization and the structure of society. Such relationships are being brought into the analysis in the rather sweeping concepts of socialism and capitalism as stages of economic development as they were elaborated by Karl Marx and Werner Sombart.

One way of looking at Marxist economics is to view it as a theory of the historical trends of economic development. Historical materialism (*histomat*) claims to be an interpretation of history in material—i.e., economic—terms. In its view religious and cultural values prevailing at any given time are merely a superstructure, a defense mechanism or a rationalization of the status quo of control of private proprietors over the means of production. Now dialectical materialism (*diamat*), the second basic concept of orthodox Marxism-Leninism, asserts that all reality, physical as well as social, is evolving in a triad. This triad consists of an existing basic situation or state which eventually produces counterforces. The initial situation or thesis will be superseded inevitably by a new one in which the contradictions—antithesis—will have gained so much strength as to assert itself. The dialectical progression is actually leading to a synthesis in which elements of the thesis and antithesis are blended and produce a higher form of reality.

Economic history is fitted by Marxism into this rather tortured scheme. Various phases of development are distinguished not according to the differentiation of sectors and functions of the economy as is done in the phases-and-stages approach, but in forms of "systems" according to the prevalence of forms of ownership. Hence we have feudalism, characterized by big landlordism; capitalism as private ownership of industrial production systems; socialism as social ownership of land and capital. It was one of the basic ideas of classical Marxism that there was an inevitability to this dialectical pattern of the historical progression of economic systems toward socialism. Once socialism was reached, no further changes in the economic structure were anticipated. Actually, this view implies a vision of collective existence in a posthistorical phase of mankind. If such a doctrine sounds strange, we may remind the reader that John Stuart Mill also visualized an end state of the economy which, however far advanced industrially, would eventually become stationary and unchanging.

*Capital,** Marx's main effort in the field of economics does not deal with socialism but a study of the "process of capitalist production." The capitalistic system is seen as continously expanding because surpluses are used to increase the accumulation of capital. In the course of these developments, transformations in the structure of capital were anticipated by Marx a considerable time before they began to assume impressive dimensions toward the end of the nineteenth century. Marx was correct in forecasting trends toward centralization and monopoly in industry, the elimination of many independent small firms, and an ever-increasing proportion of capital relative to labor. He was wrong in predicting that such changes would lead to "pauperization" of industrial workers and former middle-class people to the point where social tensions would become so great that the capitalist form of production would be replaced by its antithesis, socialism. Marx's view of economic history is that there exists an irrepressible trend toward industrialization and that industrialization inevitably leads to socialism. In this view the coming of socialism was predicated on the prior realization of high levels of output, technological advance, and scientific business management. In the old days certain socialists held that capitalism would unintentionally produce workers and

*Karl Marx, *Capital*, New York, Modern Library, Inc.

managers with sufficient know-how to operate efficiently once industry had been nationalized and the capitalist expropriated. That is to say socialism was visualized as a structural transformation of a system which was already highly advanced and industrialized. While classical Marxism is basically a theory that attempts to show that socialism in the course of economic development becomes inevitable, it does not, however, consider socialism as an instrumentality of economic development but rather its end product.

In reality, economic development in the Soviet Union has not followed this pattern. The bootstrap model emphasizing planning, priority on social overhead cost, heavy industry, and imposing austerity on consumers was the actual way of "building socialism." The rallying cry popularized under Stalin and continued with some verbal modifications in subsequent regimes to the effect that the Soviet Union must overtake and then surpass capitalism was actually an acknowledgment of economic backwardness combined with the hope for some kind of future prosperity under socialism that would be comparable to that currently enjoyed under capitalism. This was a significant modification of the original Marxist concept of the role of economic development in the coming of socialism. Official communist terminology today is, therefore, forced to present socialism as a transitional phase between capitalism and communism. Under communism there will be an equilization of income to satisfy all socially recognized needs of individuals and families. Under socialism it is conceded that vast differentials exist in earnings and living standards among various occupational groupings. Today it is being said that communism is predicated on economic development during the socialist period in the course of which a system producing abundance—an affluent society—has been established.

In his approach to economic history, Marx stressed more than his predecessors the significance of the surrounding social structure on economic change. But in linking socialism to a prior advance in industrialization, Marx was operating strictly within a social framework valid only in mid-nineteenth century Western Europe with its conviction that the type of progress achieved there would inevitably spread with identical patterns to the rest of the world. Actually, the economic development in the Western world did not lead to socialism but to a vastly modified capitalistic system. On the other hand, where socialism was introduced it occurred as a sudden transition from precapitalist to postcapitalist structures.

Like Marx, Werner Sombart,* the great historian and analyst of the capitalist system, considers aspects of the social structure. He emphasizes

*Der moderne Kapitalismus, 1902.

the fact that this system is viable only under conditions of continuous expansion. He posits all-pervasive economic development as a necessary element in the survival of this system. As we will note later, he clearly foresaw at the beginning of the present century a condition that is rapidly becoming the main concern of economists in already developed countries. Sombart stressed that capitalism as an ever-expanding system was supported by the motive of acquisition as an end in itself as it developed in modern times. He differentiates this type of behavior from the basic concern with economic and social status maintenance which according to him was characteristic of the Middle Ages and generally of traditional society. These are simplifications but Sombart was basically correct to emphasize that a historical study of economic behavior patterns shows significant differences between various periods. The profit motive appears under different forms and the way it was being treated in classical and even more recent economics was an oversimplification.

The preceding brief discussion of approaches to economic history has shown that a consideration of historical conditions is indispensable in order to place models and policies of economic development in their proper setting. On the other hand, we have seen that approaches to economic history, when applied to analyses and even to forecasts of economic development, have proven to be erroneous—or, as in the case of Marxism, almost counterindicative. It is necessary, therefore, to attempt another approach to the inescapable task imposed upon social scientists today of fashioning workable tools for the conceptualization of economic development in which proper weight is given to economic as well as historical and social patterns.

HISTORICAL AND SYSTEMATIC ASPECTS OF ECONOMIC DEVELOPMENT

For an adequate understanding of the basic and typical elements underlying economic development it is necessary to examine the historical and systematic aspects of society in a state of change and growth. There can be no economic development without accumulation of surpluses used for expansion. This accumulation requires effective cooperation of the factors of land, labor, capital, and management. Although these factors must be present whenever economic development occurs, more specific models have to be constructed to show how they are actually combined and put in operation.

A generalized historical study of the social structures of factor use and management is one phase of model building in the conceptualization of economic development. A second phase consists in the working out of different historical patterns of economic institutions and growth of the system. Economic development is at any given time the product of a mix of these two aspects. Prior to the Industrial Revolution economics activities were labor-intensive. The tools or capital used in farming and in the workshops of artisans and merchants were quantitatively insignificant apart from inventories. Labor was by far the preponderant factor in the capital-labor ratio. However, even prior to the Industrial Revolution a slow accumulation of capital and wealth occurred especially with merchants and bankers and through the rise of urban land values. For this reason, funds were available for investment in the new enterprises and industries created by the rapid advance of technology which started in the eighteenth century. However, industrialization up to the beginning of the twentieth century was concentrated in Northwestern Europe, in the United States, and in Japan. Russia prior to the takeover by the Communists in 1917 was still a predominantly agricultural country with only modest beginnings of an industrial sector. In fact, in the last third of the twentieth century industrialization is still weakest precisely in those areas where population pressures are strongest. The need to industrialize seems to be particularly urgent in these parts of the globe. However, in many of these areas the accumulation of labor and the use of labor-intensive methods of production are still the predominant characteristic of the economic structure. Designs for economic development of these areas must take this into account. The social setting, in fact the state of mind of these emerging countries must be understood in terms of their history of accumulation of labor which is so entirely different from the point of departure for accelerated economic development of systems with a background of the slow accumulation over centuries of capital. In order to facilitate the understanding of the history of accumulation given in the next chapter, a schematic presentation of the main patterns of accumulation according to the predominance of labor accumulation or capital accumulation appears on page 30.

All systems of necessity started out with accumulation of labor. But in the Western world due to the unique structure of the medieval town, independent middle classes developed that are not found in other civilizations. They were the dynamic force behind the accumulation of capital and the acceleration of economic development. This speed up in economic development took place even while the feudal system with its compulsory use of labor continued in the countryside. Eventually the middle class became the predominant economic and political force in modern Western society.

Accumulation Systems

Accumulation of Labor	Accumulation of Capital
Land utilization through serfs, tenants, slaves. Feudalism plantation economies.	Rise of cities independent of outside power structures.
Extensive farming, One-crop economies.	Rise of independent guilds of merchants and artisans. Appearance of banks and professional people.
Low rate of capital investment in land. Often large-scale unproductive public construction.	Gradual build-up of savings and investment.
Atrophied middle classes underdeveloped craft and merchant enterprises.	Differentiation of economic activities. Wholesale and retail trade.
Polarization of property distribution and income.	Gradual increase in size of enterprises.
Extremes of wealth and poverty.	Acceleration of development through industrialization.
High-level liberal education for the few. Widespread illiteracy of the many.	Compulsory public education.
Low rate of economic development, if any.	Leveling off of income differentials through the increase in middle income groups.

Accumulation of land and labor or of capital will not occur without expectations of rewards and gains from these efforts. However, the concept of "profit motive" as the all-embracing incentive for investment conceals the very great difference in economic behavior patterns in various types of economic structures. Motivation in predominantly land-labor accumulation systems are not identical with those in capital-accumulation structures.

Those who control land and labor certainly are striving to obtain large revenues. However, in most of these systems there is a certain disdain for business activity. They do not rate very high on the scale of social prestige. The main emphasis and motivation in such a social setting is status maintenance and aggrandizement. Very often there is no clear separation between public offices, duties, and revenues and the more private interests of administrators. Hence in such systems an appointment to a government post very often carries with it the assumption that the jobholder will be able to take care of his own economic requirements in addition to fulfilling certain obligations to the government.

In capital-accumulation systems the motivation focuses more exclusively on maximum monetary returns. In fully developed capitalism profits are significant not so much because they add to the scale of living and the self- and social esteem of the entrepreneur, but because they can be used for the expansion of the size of the enterprise. As this system assumes the form of a corporation state characterized by the predominance of large-scale private enterprise intimately related to the public sector, profit motivations become depersonalized. But precisely in this form they can be powerful levers for further economic development.

So far in this section we have stressed the need to conceptualize historical patterns of factor use as an essential underpinning of a comprehensive approach to economic development. In addition to this analysis of patterns of factor use, we must also consider the various types of economic growth and development of an economic system. These are the systematic, as distinct from the historical aspects of economic development.

Economic growth can occur under entirely different systematic conditions. It can be (1) sectoral growth characterized by *factor Multiplication*, or (2) structural change characterized by *factor transformation.*

Sectoral growth has occurred over long periods of economic history. It is characterized by an expansion of already existing sectors of the economy such as farming and urban markets into larger proportions—without, however, bringing about fundamental changes in economic techniques and targets. Thus the conversion of primeval forests into farming areas and the founding of new towns characteristic of early medieval European economic history would be of the sectoral-growth type.

Factor transformation is linked up with advances in technology. It is characteristic of maturing economies and brings about the rise of new industries, the increase in labor productivity, declining labor requirements in agricultural and industrial production and a rising demand for better-trained office and managerial employees. Structural changes of this type cause a realignment of the sectors of the economy, changes in rural-urban ratio of the population and a growth in the service sector, and expansion of the educational system and of public facilities and services.

We have now outlined four aspects of economic development. Two of them refer to the processes of accumulation; two are concerned with patterns of growth of the economic system. Accumulation patterns, often going back far into history, are of great contemporary significance for the outlook of further economic development. Designs for such development and formulation of policies must be based on a definition of the conditions at the point of departure in which such historical aspects must be considered. Only then can a decision be made whether sectoral growth or factor transformation is the suitable procedure. In actuality every situation in economic development will represent a mix of accumulation and developmental conditions. Just what this mix is in concrete situations must be decided by analytical procedures that attempt to ascertain the weight of the four points outlined here concerning accumulation and growth patterns. If sufficient information could ever be gathered dealing with the quantitative aspects of these complex historical, social, and economic configurations and the time factors associated with them in terms of leads and lags, it would be possible to computerize these data and utilize them according to such data embodied in a particular scenario of economic development.

In this text we will, however, stress the verbal approach, which will remain of value if the problems of economic development are to be handled not only by quantitative yardsticks with all their advantages and pitfalls but also by prudential judgments based on comprehensive understanding. These qualities of decision making—that is, the method of understanding—will always remain indispensable. Denying this would be tantamount to believing in social mechanics, an early nineteenth-century ideology that should be discarded as we approach the twenty-first.

Chapter 2 deals with some concepts and the predominant historical patterns of accumulation of land, labor and capital. In Chapter 3 the systematic aspects of economic development is analyzed in greater detail. Chapter 4 shows that development theory and policy is encountering some paradoxes which present great challenges to contemporary economics. Against this background development problems in certain areas of the world will be discussed in some detail.

chapter **2**

Historical Forms of Accumulation of Land, Labor, and Capital

Modern economic systems are market oriented and assume that such factors of production as land, labor, and capital are available to whoever has the purchasing power to acquire them and to use them in various combinations to offer goods and services to the consumer. Even centralized planning systems such as the Soviet economy are tending toward "market socialism", steering away from rigid regimentation of the output and design of consumer goods. Capitalistic countries, especially the United States with its huge aggregate public demand for defense and space items produced by private industry, retain in principle the institutions of a free-factor market.

If we have this modern economic structure in mind in which capital accumulation and continuous expansion through additional investment shape the growth path it is easy to overlook that historically speaking there have been other forms of the accumulation of factors. In fact the greater part of economic history is characterized not by the accumulation of capital or the conversion of savings into investment but by the accumulation of land. Through accumulation of land and the appropriation of labor of people "acquired" along with the titles to land, accumulated labor becomes a prime factor of production and the basis of political power, economic status, and great wealth. These methods of accumulation through the control and the systematic use of labor have accounted in many periods of history for an extensive economic development. We encounter here patterns of development that do not presuppose prior savings but a seizure and distribution of power by ruling groups, enabling them to embark on a course of economic development such as we encounter in antiquity in the "hydraulic states" of the Near East. It follows that the very important concept of a *low-productivity trap* in which retarded economies find themselves has not always been a bar to economic development in history. Even in the twentieth century much economic development—for instance in Communist China—stems from a massive use of the abundantly available factor labor. Ragnar Nurkse* has made a valuable contribution to our understanding of the impasse faced by many underdeveloped countries as a result of low productivity, lack of capital, inability to save or to invest, and the resulting inability to initiate processes of development. But this low-productivity trap refers only to that type of economic development that is predicated on the accumulation of capital. While this is the predominant pattern in many parts of the world today it is not the only one. In fact the "bootstrap system" of economic development mentioned in Chapter 1 relies to a large extent on the large-scale use of cheap labor.

Proper weight must be given to the fact that historically factors of production were rarely as free as they are presented in contemporary models of the economic structure. The free market of these factors when it came into full operation with the formal abolition of the privileged economic status of feudalism in the countryside and the craft and merchant guilds in the cities showed for a long time the aftereffects of former monopolies on factor use and of the many restrictions on competition. The early classical economists did not allow for these institutional structures. They assumed that free competition could repeal long-standing historical economic inequalities in a short period of time.

This nonhistorical frame of classical economic theory led to a theoretical impasse. On the one side it was stressed that profits were the most powerful motive for the accumulation of capital and hence for economic growth and development. On the other side it was not possible to show how profits could originate within the exchange process. It was argued that profits are somehow being created because they were needed as an incentive for capital formation. Even in this context the classical economists took a gloomy view of the long-run outlook of economic development. Assuming that the law of decreasing returns would assert itself evermore as the scale of economic operations increased, they visualized an end phase of stagnation in which profits would drop to zero.

Marx's critique of the classical theory of accumulation and of profit is based on an income-flow argument. He asserted that in the exchange process of a capitalistic system profits would cancel each other out. Hence he concluded that the cause of profits and of accumulation of wealth must lie outside the circular flow of a market system. This argument is not valid,

*Ragnar Nurkse, *Equilibrium and Growth in the World Economy*, Cambridge, Mass., Harvard University Press, 1961, p. 242.

however, except for the hypothetical case of a system which at the same time is perfectly competitive and completely stationary. An advancing system even if it comes close to the perfectly competitive model will always offer profit opportunities to those individuals and firms which move ahead of others to newly developing areas and economic frontiers. On a more generalized level, the social structures, particularly the impact of power relations on economic realtions, is of paramount significance for the understanding of problems of economic development. Economic development requires accumulation of productive assets. Accumulation in turn cannot be viewed out of context with the various forms of control of labor and of capital.

Prior to the Industrial Revolution which set in about three hundred years ago, the main source of wealth and of income was land; capital played a minor role. Furthermore, land produced income not only because of the revenues that could be gained from it through agricultural operations, but more important was the fact that control over land also meant control over people attached to estates and land holdings. Labor was the most important and most valuable factor of production. Prior to the rise of modern industry, labor accounted for by far the largest proportion of the capital-labor ratio. To gain control of labor and to marshal it toward such economic development goals as the building of irrigation systems, canals, roads, warehouses and other large structures was for the greater part of history a prerequisite for expansion and advance. In recent centuries the factor capital and the methods of its accumulation have begun to outrank labor especially in advanced countries. This trend has brought about profound changes in the educational and training requirements of labor and has improved its economic condition. In order to analyze the impact of these historical patterns in greater detail, we now present separate outlines of the history of accumulation of labor and of capital.

ACCUMULATION OF LABOR

As long as prehistoric man was following a nomadic way of life without permanent settlement, there was no systematic use of human beings in the service of others. Often members of "foreign" or "enemy" groups were slain and eaten by the victors. One is almost tempted to say that in these primitive stages of strife and struggle, human beings were utilized by others not for production purposes, but as items for the satisfaction of biological and deeply rooted psychological needs and superstitions. When agriculture was introduced and stone-age villages set up, a certain degree of equality came to exist between the inhabitants. They did not yet separate into distinct classes of masters, serfs, and slaves. However, at the point of transition from prehistory to history we already encounter a rigidly strati-fied society. The large mass of the people in Egypt and in the Near East empires worked on the land and had to deliver crops to the rulers. They were subject to compulsory labor draft. Without the availability of large numbers of laborers from the population the massive works of construc-tion characteristic of these early states could not have been carried out. It is of great importance to understand in what manner the rather unstruc-tured primitive society of the prehistoric age changed into these domina-tion-submission patterns. If we gain an insight into this process we also have a key to the widespread historical pattern of the accumulation of la-bor in the form of *serfdom* and *slavery*.

These two forms of unfree labor can exist only in a social setting in which one group of people, the masters and landowners share in a power structure permitting them to exercise rights over those subject to their command and which elevate them high above the status of manual work-ers. In fact, the disdain for manual work which is running through many civilizations and is still apparent today in the desire of many people to achieve at least white-collar status, is rooted in the past where a great deal of the more simple manual work was done by unfree labor.

There are significant differences between the institutions of serfdom and of slavery. Both have in common an important economic characteris-tic: they supply free labor to those who can claim their services.

Serfdom is a form of unfree labor mostly connected with manorial estates in feudalistic society. Feudalism is one of the most universal social and economic institutions. It is an elaborate arrangement between title-holders of the estate and the farm population inhabiting its area. *Tenants* are people bound to the estate but holding plots of land which they can work for their own account after having made deliveries in kind or paid rent to the manorial owner. *Serfs* are inhabitants of the estate not owning such plot to any extent.

Typically the system makes free labor services available for stated periods of time to be rendered to the lord by tenants. Serfs are subject to virtually unrestricted employment by their masters. Tenancy having its origin in feudalism but surviving in many parts of the world today is a somewhat milder form of unfree labor in agricultural settings. Villagers on estates are often sharecroppers, having to pay a considerable percentage of their crops to the landlord either in kind or in its money equivalent.

Frequently they are in continual debt to him to repay him for advances in seeds and other necessities. As long as feudalism was a legally established system tenants like serfs were obligated to labor services although on a more limited scale. Furthermore they were also subject to restraints on freedom to move especially to leave the estate for cities.

Feudalism prevailed in China during the period of the Warring States from the eighth to the third century B.C. It was liquidated with the establishment of the centralized imperial state with its bureaucratic government which came into being in the third century B.C. The period of the founding of towns in the ancient world or the process of *synoikism* was preceded by a long period of feudalism in Greece and in Central Italy evolving from the invasion of Greece and Italy by Indo-Germanic tribes prior to 1000 B.C. While free farmers were not unknown in this age, patrician landholders were able to develop their feudalistic structures. In the ancient world, the transfer of political power from rural clan rule to urban patricians changed the character of that society, creating citizenship also for people not descended from patricians. When the Roman Empire collapsed in the fifth century A.D. and the power center again shifted to the countryside, a new phase of feudalism as the paramount political and social institution arose in the Western world.

As a rule, the origin of serfdom is political rather than economic. In Chinese antiquity intruders from the Northwest equipped with chariots invaded village settlements in the many river valleys and imposed their rule. The peasant population was required to render labor services to feudal lords and later to territorial princes while continuing to work on land which they had already opened up for agriculture. Similar patterns were applied by the Indo-Germanic tribes invading Greece and Italy. When feudalism was revived at the end of the West Roman Empire, somewhat different patterns occurred occasionally. When the Saxons invaded Britain they cleared parts of eastern and southern England of the resident population and set up homogeneous village communities. But eventually, these old communities of free and equal peasants developed a class structure. Those who participated in military campaigns under the king were rewarded with additional land grants. Huge tracts of land were also given by the king to monastic orders. With this development, serfdom again made its appearance and actually continued in the Western world to the end of the eighteenth century.

Within the overall structure of the feudal estate, the serfs were that group of workers who had little or no land of their own. Tenants usually owned more land, although in Europe landlords saw to it that tenant farmers did not acquire too much contiguous land. Tenant holdings were frequently in scattered, narrow strips. However, as long as the feudal system lasted, rural populations were subject, not only to labor services to be rendered to their lord; they also had to be available for work organized under the auspices of territorial authorities. While this was not a significant factor in the total labor obligations of the rural population during the Middle Ages, it became more significant in the seventeenth century. At that time governments became concerned in Europe with large-scale improvement projects such as road and canal building, draining of marshy areas and general upgrading of the countryside. When under the policies of mercantilism factories were set up in rural areas, attempts were made to force local people to work there. It is easy to see then that a great resentment developed against the *corvée* or the subjecting of rural populations to forced labor. This economic institution of very long standing was abolished only in the course of the French Revolution of 1789.

While early in the sixteenth century, the enslavement of native Indians was outlawed in the new vice-kingdoms of Spain in Central and South America, the feudal institution of serfdom was transmitted to the New World creating the class of *peons* which are the serfs of the New World. Land grants were given by the King of Spain under the name of *encommuniendas,* entrusting not only the soil but the resident population to the recipient of this feudal award. Again the principle was applied that this rural population was liable to a draft as laborers on construction and other projects. The chances for these people to acquire sufficient land to gain economic independence were extremely limited and for centuries they have continued to live as marginal sharecroppers.

Serfdom was also the predominant form of agricultural labor in Eastern Europe, especially in imperial Russia. This condition of labor was terminated only in 1861. The main effect of the abolition of rural serfdom here and elsewhere was the creation of a greater measure of mobility of rural people. They could escape the economic trap in which they had found themselves for generations under feudalism. Actually it was this group that provided the manpower for the rapidly growing factory system in Western Europe. A great many nineteenth-century immigrants to the United States also came from areas where feudalism had been the predominant economic institution up to recently. Although the institution of serfdom was widespread throughout economic history in many parts of the world, it is important to distinguish it clearly from slavery. Serfs, while obligated to render labor services to landlords or government were free in the sense that they could neither be bought nor sold. They were attached to the soil and stayed on when there was a change of title. Custom also established their right to reside on the estate in return for their rendering of the labor services. Slaves, or course, were treated analogous to commodities and could be acquired or disposed of in slave markets. Before we turn our attention to this form of labor, we can sum up this brief survey of serfdom by stressing that this institution was a widespread technique in the process of accumulating wealth. The control of land automatically implied the control of the people—that is, the factor labor—who were connected with it. It was not without reason that landowners in eighteenth- and early nineteenth-century Russia measured their wealth in terms of the number of "souls" which they owned in the villages on their estates.

The main effect of this system of accumulating wealth through the control of unfree labor over many generations is the development of great discrepancies in the distribution of land. In most Latin American countries, but also in Eastern Europe prior to the World Wars and in Near Eastern countries such as Iran, a minute fraction of the population owned by far the greatest proportion of land.* Furthermore, since labor was cheap and abundant, this latifundia system did not create incentives for capital investments in farm machinery and modern fertilizers. In many parts of the world the concentration of landownership in the hands of the few favored the growth of monocultures—one-crop systems of farming producing such staples as sugar, tobacco, cotton, coffee, and rubber. Very often latifundia were administered by managers on behalf of absentee landowners, as in Southern Italy and Spain. Even after the formal abolishment of serfdom, labor supply remained so abundant in many areas dominated by big land holdings that the possibility to use officially free labor as a continued source of the accumulation of wealth persisted.

Frequently absentee landowners would invite entrepreneurs to submit bids to obtain the right to manage the estate for a given period of time. These administrators would promise to pay an annual money amount to the landowner. In return, he would try to run the estate so as to obtain the highest possible profit in excess over the rent he had pledged himself to pay to the owner. It is obvious that this system, continued into the twentieth century, discouraged intensive farming and crop diversification. At the same time, one-crop agriculture is bound to generate chronic underemployment, supplying rural populations only with a limited period of gainful work during the year. Since in most parts of the world where such conditions continued even after the formal disestablishment of feudalism,

*Details are given later in this section.

alternate employment opportunities are lacking. The impact of long-standing historical labor arrangement of feudalism continued virtually into the present time. Land reform, especially distribution of land to the rural population in order to make it more self-supporting and independent has been on the agenda of many countries characterized by concentration of land ownership and absentee landlordism for a long period of time. We will see in Chapter 4 that realization of such reform programs, while desirable, is no longer the answer to the urgent necessity to liquidate survivals and remnants of feudal labor relations and conditions.

Slavery is the second system of supplying free labor services which can be used for the accumulation of wealth. Actually, wherever slave markets develop the master must lay out money in order to purchase a slave. Furthermore, he must maintain slaves in a physical condition good enough to enable them to work with a certain measure of efficiency and productivity. Compared to feudal serfdom this use of the factor labor seems to be rather uneconomical. While the master can claim the full-time services of a slave, in contrast to the more restricted time that tenants have to allocate to the lord, the total dependence of the slave makes it necessary for the master to provide a minimum level of material support to his slaves. But unlike tenants and serfs, a slave-labor supply was frequently not reproductive. Hence in order to maintain slavery, it was necessary to keep sources of slave labor supply flowing throughout the centuries. In antiquity, as well as in the modern age, slave trade was therefore a significant and usually highly profitable branch of commerce.

Despite the built-in cost and inefficiency of the use of the factor labor in the form of slavery, this labor system was widely used at differing degrees throughout most of history. One of the main origins of slavery is the claim of victors to services of a vanquished people, including the right to sell some of their members into slavery. Another source of slavery was the surrender of debtors to creditors. Still another source practiced in China as well as in Europe up to the seventeenth century was the selling of children. While the institution of slavery was widely established, there are vast historical differences in its concept and in its operation especially if we compare the Roman system to that which developed in the West Indies and in the North American colonies in the seventeenth century.

Slavery was firmly defined and regulated under Roman law. There were model contracts dealing with the purchase of a slave. Most important there was a clearly established procedure for the freeing of a slave by his masters, called manumission. In antiquity, the employment of slaves was by no means restricted to agriculture. It ranged over the whole gamut of jobs from private tutors of the children of wealthy Romans to the most menial tasks. In Greece and Rome slaves were not only employed by private masters but also in such state enterprises as mines. Most of the heavy labor in construction and in maintenance was carried out by slaves. Slavery supplied the broad base on which the pyramid of free occupations of artisans, shopkeepers, merchants, and landowners was erected. Slaves were used in mass production, such as the multiplication of manuscripts through the method of dictation or in ceramic products and similar items of mass consumption. They provided the motive power in galleys. However, throughout the period of Roman history the principle was strictly maintained that only free men could serve in the Roman army.

The steady expansion of Rome from its assertion of hegemony over its immediate neighbors in Central Italy in the fourth century B.C. to the imposing world empire in the first century A.D. increased the flow of slave labor into the Roman economy. The patricians, who had retained their landed estates even after they had moved to the city of Rome and established a senatorial regime, took advantage of this cheap labor supply. Gradually the feudal structure of these land holdings was changed into a plantation system using slaves. With it came the development of such crops as olives for oil and grapes for wine, accompanied by a sharp decline in the growing of grains in Italy. Increasingly grain was produced in slave-operated plantations in Africa and in Sicily. With the growth of the plantation system, the free small farmers who had been able to maintain themselves in the earlier phases of Roman history, experienced ever-increasing difficulties. Many moved to the city so that beginning in the first century A.D., a depopulation of the countryside was notable. The slave economy favored the rise of the latifundia and contributed to the polarization of wealth on the one side and poverty on the other in the Roman Empire.

Eventually the sources of labor supply began to run dry in Rome. Once the period of imperial expansion had come to an end, the possibility of laying claim to the manpower of vanquished people was greatly reduced. Furthermore, many masters saw great advantages in freeing slaves by making them partners in business enterprises which they themselves did not want to conduct. Slaves could acquire freedom by obligating themselves to make favorable arrangements with their former masters. If we also take into account the fact, already alluded to, that slave populations are usually not self-reproducing, it is easy to see why one of the great problems besetting the Roman Empire in the third century A.D. was a growing labor shortage. The labor force as a whole, slave and free, was no longer sufficient to maintain the operations of the Roman economy in the vast imperial framework which had been established in the first two centuries of the Empire. Too much of the resources had been invested in nonproductive, nonself-sustaining projects such as monumental public buildings of all kinds. This type of accumulation of sterile wealth presupposed the continuous availability of slave labor. When this condition no longer prevailed, the Roman economy, because it was topheavy, began to disintegrate. The Emperor Diocletian (284-305 A.D.) tried to stop this trend. An attempt to stabilize prices and to control inflation by imperial edict failed. More effective was a ban on free movement of the population, especially from the open countryside to the city. Serfdom made its reappearance in rural estates as slavery lost its economic significance.

In the ensuing centuries, unfree labor in form of serfs and tenants obligated to certain labor services became the predominant labor system on the countryside. The citizens of the towns which developed in the early Middle Ages were free. The power of the feudal lords ended at the city gates and kings and emperors assumed the burden of protecting this freedom of cities. The institution of slavery fell into disuse. The fact that in documents serfs were often referred to with the Roman name for slave *servus* should not mislead us into assuming that slavery was a significant element in the economic structure of the Middle Ages in Europe. Only with the discovery of the New World was there a large-scale revival of the use of slave manpower. But by now the terms and the social treatment of slavery had changed fundamentally from the conditions to be encountered in antiquity. One new element was the difference in race between masters and slaves. Whereas in antiquity masters and slaves belonged in the overwhelming majority of cases to minor variations of the white race, making prima facie physical identification of slaves virtually impossible, the situation was entirely different when the large-scale importation of slaves from Africa to the New World got under way in the middle of the sixteenth century. The revival of slavery as a source of labor supply and as a means for the accumulation of wealth was predicated on the outlawing of the enslavement of the native Indian population in the New World. They were largely held in the status of serfs. Another reason for the large-scale use of Africans was the rapid growth of the plantation economy based on sugar and tobacco in the West Indies. Indians proved to be unwilling and unsuitable for the type of work required in this form of farming.

Unlike the slaves of antiquity whose status was often derived from their membership in a vanquished nation, the African slaves were purchased by merchants from Northern Europe from native chiefs. A highly profitable triangular trade developed. Boats with a cargo of trinkets and other cheap merchandise desired by African rulers would go from ports in Britain, the Netherlands, and France to the west coast of Africa. Here the European wares were exchanged against slaves. These were packed into the boats under incredibly inhumane and unsanitary conditions. During the Atlantic crossings a considerable proportion of the Africans succumbed to these hardships. Those who survived were auctioned off in slave markets, especially in the Caribbean Islands. The first cargo of slaves destined for the North American colonies arrived in Jamestown, Virginia, in 1619.

While slavery in modern times showed these basic differences with slavery in antiquity discussed in the preceding paragraphs, a further differentiation in the actual operation of the system was brought about by the different legal tradition of the Spanish and Portuguese and of the Anglo-Saxons. The former were aware of their Roman law background in which slavery was a clearly defined legal institution. Hence from an early stage, manumission, the freeing of slaves was practiced on a considerable scale, especially in Brazil. In the English colonies this tradition was unknown, and the treatment of slaves was even more harsh there than in Latin America. But in South as well as North America the main employment of slaves was in agriculture and in domestic services. The diversification of work of slaves characteristic of the ancient world did not develop in more recent history.

Slave-operated sugar plantations became a highly profitable enterprise especially as long as the price of sugar was held artificially high by mercantilistic policies of the home countries. Tobacco plantations also became a source of wealth due to the rapidly rising demand for tobacco in Europe, where it had been unknown prior to the discovery of the New World. Toward the end of the eighteenth century, stimulated by the introduction of the cotton gin, cotton plantations requiring huge numbers of slaves began to develop, creating considerable wealth for their owners in a comparatively short period of time.

However, by that time an abolitionist movement had already started in England soon to be followed by the demand to stop the spread of slavery in the United States and terminate this economic institution completely. In 1832 slavery was abolished in the British Empire. In 1848 it was terminated in the French West Indies, in 1863 in the United States, and in 1888 in Brazil.

By the end of the nineteenth century compulsory labor systems seemed to have disappeared throughout the world. Slavery had been abolished and freedom of movement introduced, thereby making it possible for former serfs or slaves to leave the countryside and to accept free-labor contracts wherever the opportunity offered. However, the abolishment of legal and economic institutions does not repeal automatically the social and economic effects they have had over long periods of time. Furthermore there remained and there still exists today large "gray areas" between compulsory labor and free labor. An example may be found in the following brief account of what happened in the former British colonies of Trinidad and Guyana after the termination of slavery in 1832.

Trinidad had been largely neglected by the Spaniards. In the eighteenth century French planters came to the island from French possessions in the Caribbeans which had been taken over by the British at the end of the Seven Years' War. They started sugar plantations. When the British took over Trinidad during the Napoleonic wars, the plantation system was expanded and the number of Negro slaves increased. When slavery was abolished, the plantation owners expected the former slaves to stay with them as agricultural laborers. However, many of the former slaves escaped into the undeveloped hinterlands where they took up subsistence farming as squatters. A great labor shortage developed. In those days of imperial power a way out was found without much delay. Workers from East India were brought to these American colonies of the British under seven-year contracts of indenture. This is the reason why today a somewhat precarious political balance prevails in these two former British colonies between the African and the East Indian segments of the population.

This brief survey of the history of the accumulation of wealth through the accumulation and control of labor shows that in the preindustrial age this form of factor use was an important aspect of economic development. The end result of this type of development was, however, a high degree of maldistribution of wealth, the consolidation of a small, prosperous, and often highly educated upper class on one end of the scale and a rapidly growing indigent and largely illiterate population on the other. In many parts of the world the effects of this type of compulsory employment of labor survived into the twentieth century and can be seen very clearly in patterns of land distribution and class structure, for instance in Latin America.

A study by Thomas F. Carroll* offers highly illuminating details in support of the preceding statement. Around 1950, it was estimated that for Latin America as a whole 1.5 percent of the agricultural units held 64.9 percent of the land area whereas 72.6 percent of the farms had to share in 3.7 percent of the land area. It is obvious then that the majority

*See: The Land Reform Issue in Latin America in A.O. Hirschman Latin American Issues Twentieth Century Fund 1961.

of "farmers," former peons or slaves were engaged in subsistence farming yielding an extremely low income. Studies of individual countries show the same pattern in an even more accentuated manner. In Venezuela 1.6 percent of the farms accounted for 74 percent of the acreage and 88 percent, the midget farms, had only 5.4 percent of land at their disposal. In Bolivia 6 percent of the farms accounted for 92 percent of the land area whereas 78 percent of the farms had only 1 percent of the total acreage. More recent figures from Guadeloupe, French West Indies, which had a typical colonial background as a one-crop colonial economy shows similar conditions.* In 1967, fifty-one agricultural enterprises owned 40 percent of the arable land whereas 13,861 "farms" had an average size of less than 2.5 acres. More recently, large-scale growing of bananas has been added to create greater diversification of agriculture in the West Indies. In Guadeloupe 10 percent of the banana plantations accounted for 66 percent of all the land used for this crop.

Mexico did not differ from other Latin American countries in this pattern of land distribution. In that country, however, peonage of native Indians rather than African slave labor was the pattern of accumulation of wealth through the accumulation of land and labor. However, early in the twentieth century, with the overthrow of President Diaz in 1911, structural changes were introduced by the Party of Revolutionary Institutions which has succeeded to establish a stable, basically one-party political system. There has been a considerable distribution of land from latifundia to small farmers. But in 1950 42.2 percent of the total farm population still was in the category of landless farm workers and the population as a whole was increasing at an annual rate of more than 3 percent.

While the use of unfree labor was a feature of feudalism and plantation systems in many parts of the world, the situation of the large rural masses freed from the constraint of these structures, once they had been officially abolished differed very widely according to the overall stage of development of the various countries. In fact it is this difference in the opportunities available to newly freed rural populations in Western Europe and the situation in which masses found themselves, for instance in Latin America, once peonage and slavery had been formally terminated that presents one of the root problems of economic development today.

As will be shown in greater detail in the next section, feudalism did not prevent in Europe the rise of a substantial middle class of master

---

*Quoted from an extensive four-part analytical report by Charles Vanhecke. The section of the report quoted here was published in Le Monde, December 22, 1967.

craftsmen, merchants, and shopkeepers who were able to engage in economic activities on a level of independence. Furthermore, the formal termination of feudalism and the introduction of a great measure of labor mobility and freedom of contract coincided with the first Industrial Revolution developing around the steam engine. A study of internal and international migration during the nineteenth century shows clearly that the new industrial workers manning the textile mills, coal mines, and steel mills came to a large degree from those areas where there prevailed a large concentration of big land holdings. Miners and steel workers in the Ruhr district in Germany, in Belgium, in Northern France as well as in Pennsylvania and other parts of the United States had their origins in these areas just emerging from feudalism of the latifundia type in Eastern Germany and in Poland as well as in Southern Italy. While the reasons which led to the abolition of feudal prerogatives in Europe are complex, there is no doubt that even a partial freezing of labor supply on the open country, as at one time decreed by Emperor Diocletian, had become incompatible with the accelerating rate of industrialization and of growth with its increasing demand for labor of all kinds.

The situation was entirely different in areas where the abolition of peonage and of slavery did not coincide with early phases of industrialization. Wherever feudalism or a plantation economy was the predominant system to the exclusion of urban middle classes and the economic diversification which their presence brings about, the transition from agricultural labor to industrial employment of newly freed slaves or peons was far less immediate than in Europe at the beginning of the nineteenth century—if it was possible at all. To assume that emerging countries can with a time lag of one hundred and fifty years repeat the European and American transition from a predominantly agricultural to an industrialized society is to overlook basic differences in historical structures. A mechanical transfer of development models will not come to grips with these problems. They have to be analyzed and resolved within the historical frame of reference of specific areas, taking into account not only economic history but the still continuing impact of formerly discontinued institutions of land and labor accumulation.

One of the great differences between middle-class and feudal economic arrangements and institutions is the outlook of the decision-making leadership group. In fact, this point is so essential for the proper understanding of designs for economic development that it will be examined at length in the last section of this chapter.

ACCUMULATION OF CAPITAL

The term "capital" as used in economics is rather ambiguous. One aspect of capital can be defined in the words of Nassau Senior as "produced means of production." This refers to tools and machines or what has also been termed real capital. Capital in terms of stocks and bonds represents claims relating to real capital and the value of its output. Money as such, including savings, is not capital but merely generalized purchasing power which can be utilized for the acquisition of consumer as well as producer goods. If money and in some cases credit is used to acquire additional producer goods or land or structures erected on it, such use is called *investment*.

The formation of capital is always time-consuming and requires a diversion of at least part of the individual or social effort from the production of immediately available consumer goods to the accumulation of capital. Formation of capital can go on as an activity of individual or of private groups for their own account and benefit. Generically, however, this process also occurs in collective, planned economies operating under long-run investment plans. In this section we will be concerned primarily with the private accumulation of capital.

In the ancient empires of the Near East and Far East, cities developed and in many cases grew into considerable size. They were the centers of storage of agricultural surpluses, of worship and government. Unlike the polis of antiquity and medieval towns, these cities were not independent political units but in many cases creations of the King or ruler. The inhabitants were subject to him. However, many of the city dwellers became highly skilled artisans, craftsmen, scribes, and officials. To a large degree they were working for the requirements of the courts and the armed forces of the country. In addition there were merchants and shopkeepers. In *China* and in other Eastern countries adopting the Chinese model of civilization, skills in literacy and in literature were the prerequisites for admission to and promotion within the bureaucratic structure. Nevertheless, the vast group of people exercising what might be considered typical middle-class functions lacked the type of independence enjoyed by guild merchants and master craftsmen in the town setting of the European Middle Ages. The opportunities for the accumulation of wealth were predicated on their participation in the political power structure through administrative appointments, working for the government and its installations or the conferring of trade privileges. There developed to a certain extent a market economy, but it was never the dominant economic institution.

The polis of the *Graeco-Roman World* represents an altogether different structure, although like the Far Eastern cities it did not create a genuinely independent middle class. Most of the cities of antiquity were established by deliberate decisions of the landed gentry of a comparatively small area. They were founded by them as centers of trade and for the purpose of a concentration of political, financial, and military power. The patricians in Rome were the descendants of such founding families. They retained their land holdings outside the city walls. Eventually they converted their feudal estates where serfs had rendered labor services into plantations using slave labor and raising cash crops. Whereas in medieval Europe feudalism on the countryside and city government were entirely separate and belonged literally to different political orders or estates, the city of antiquity became the focus of a uniform power structure. The ruling class in the city claimed this status because of its feudal background. From the very beginning ancient cities attracted considerable numbers of people of heterogeneous local and national backgrounds. These inhabitants were held clearly distinct from the descendants of the founding families. However, they were free and eventually could acquire citizenship rights. In Rome this large group of people were called the *populus* or populace. They had clearly circumscribed political rights and freedom of choice with regard to occupations.

Both patricians and plebeians owned slaves who formed the third group of the urban population of ancient cities. They were employed by the craftsmen and enterprises who were the backbone of the local city economy. A great diversification of production activities took place in the ancient cities. There were the shops producing pottery, very often in large volumes for the purpose of exports; there were carpenters, wood carvers, and shipwrights. Many specialized in the production of arms such as bows. Metalworkers were, of course, particularly important in the production of helmets, swords, and protective armor. Another specialty was the production of metal mirrors. Service type businesses also developed, such as inns and taverns. Eventually retail shops were to be found in great profusion, especially in Roman cities. When in the imperial days apartment houses were erected, many of them had shops on the first floor. However, there were also large commercial structures in which merchants could rent space for their retail operations.

The ancient city is characterized by great public outlays for huge structures such as city walls, aqueducts, temples, theaters, public baths, sports arenas, and elaborate forums. Building materials were often produced by slave labor in quarries outside the city, usually operated by government. Actual construction was also carried out by slave labor. However, as a rule, the construction project itself was contracted out to private enterprises. Export and import trade, the latter especially in grains and in slaves, was also carried out in the private sector of the economy.

It is clear from the foregoing description of the range of business activity in the acient city that a great variety of economic opportunities was available to citizens in the crafts, in small shops, or in the larger affairs of building construction and foreign trade. While none of these pursuits could be carried out without slave labor, they provided for a certain accumulation of capital, especially in the form of surpluses gained by the availability of nonwage labor and windfall gains which could be made by those benefiting from their participation in or closeness to the political power structure.

The latter point is decisive for our understanding of capital accumulation in the ancient world, especially Rome. While there was a substantial class of craftsmen, shopkeepers, merchants, and contractors, the main source of wealth leading to a considerable accumulation of assets was connected with the economic benefits derived from war. We have seen in the preceding section that territorial expansion through warfare provided the main source for slave labor. Now we must turn to other aspects of this manner of the acquisition of wealth. Under the Roman system the victorious power was entitled to seize valuable land of the vanquished people and auction it off to the highest bidder, usually a Roman citizen. He could use this land for the setting up of plantations or he could resell it. This, in the words of Franz Oppenheimer, was *accumulation of wealth by political means, not by economic means.* Conquered territories also had to pay tributes or taxes to Rome, which opened up another political means for the accumulation of wealth. The collection of these taxes was farmed out to private enterprises submitting bids to the government. Naturally, they tried to gouge the hapless taxpayer in order to line their own pockets as well. Slave trade was also in private hands, thus opening up additional opportunities to profit from the political successes of the state.

Gains achieved from these activities could easily be invested in urban and rural real estate. With the onset of the imperial period in Rome we encounter the speculative tenement house builder and generally a considerable number of nouveaux riches. Below this conspicuous but rather small group we find the substantial mass of the small businessman. However most of the accumulation of wealth was directly in the public sector or derived from it.

Throughout antiquity a very large proportion of resources, labor, materials, and money was allocated to what can be called an early form of social overhead capital. In addition to the catalogue of public structures in the cities already mentioned, roads and bridges were built on a vast scale, and fortifications and permanent encampments for the legions had to be created in frontier areas. All this was reinforced by the vainglory of emperors wanting to be remembered by posterity as builders of monumental structures. When Constantine the Great ruled over Rome early in the fourth century A.D., the Roman economy was already beset by deep troubles such as an increasing labor shortage, scarcity of money, and rising insecurity in frontier regions. Nevertheless he continued the multifarious building programs on a grand scale.

If we apply to Roman economic history concepts of development the ever-deepening crisis and the eventual downfall of the Roman Empire can be traced to a faulty apportioning of factors. Accumulation of wealth in the private sector was not derived primarily from generally productive activities but from participation in the advantages accruing to political power. The tax system became ever more oppressive. The desperate attempts of Emperor Diocletian late in the third century A.D. to assure a steady flow of revenue through the introduction of the principle of collective liability for tax payments of citizens in the crafts and trades siphoned off income to such an extent that the ability of craftsmen and merchants to protect and increase their assets was undermined.

We have seen that the Roman economy is characterized by an unbalanced allocation of resources. Too much was given to the public sector for nonproductive construction activities and not enough remained for capital expansion in the private sector. As is well known, large public funds were used by the Romans to make bread available to the urban masses and to entertain them with lavish spectacles. However, it would be entirely erroneous to single those two programs out as a simplistic explanation of the downfall of ancient Rome. The root cause of this historical catastrophe is to be found in the fact that the Romans never found a way to shift from an accumulation through military and political means to an accumulation through successful activities in trade and commerce. The latter were so closely tied to the former and also predicated on the continued functioning of the institution of slavery that economic collapse became the inevitable result of the disintegration of the military-political structure of the Roman Empire.

We have thus far seen that the busy activities in the ancient cities of the Far and Near East and of antiquity did not lead to a significant accumulation of capital, able to survive changes in the political setting.

The history of accumulation in the post-Roman world of Europe is entirely different. The emerging Germanic nations who overran the Roman Empire had already a nucleus of a feudal system when they settled down in France, Spain, Italy, and the Western part of Germany. In their drives toward the West and the South they were led by dukes and the beginnings of a nobility who traveled about on horseback. The rank and file of freemen, accompanied by their women and children, followed on foot. The land taken over was distributed by the warlord or chief, who then became king, retaining a substantial part of the conquered territory as his domain. This land was the economic basis for the exercise of his rule. Large land grants were given by the king to various leaders of the nobility, and, after their conversion to Christianity, to monasteries and to bishops. On these secular and ecclesiastical estates the feudal system with its labor services required of tenants and of serfs developed and continued basically for almost one thousand years. Now, in the context of our study of the history of accumulation of capital, it is important to realize that in Western medieval society the center of power remained in the countryside. There was a certain exclusive democracy at the top of this structure because the king was considered the first among equal lords. It took many centuries of strife for them to emerge as absolute rulers on the European continent and organize effective centralized governments.

Towns were originally alien structures in this economic and political system of European feudalism. They developed in many cases at the ecclesiastical seats of bishops. Often the rural people from the surrounding countryside took shelter behind the early city walls against invaders ravaging the countryside. Eventually merchants and artisans settled in these towns and local markets developed. Now these towns were independent of territorial lords of the adjacent rural areas. This freedom was often guaranteed by town charters issued to the cities by the king. After the Norman Conquest English towns specifically asked King William to confirm their charters.

The inhabitants of the cities were free—they were not subject to any labor service or draft based on feudal relations in the rural areas. In fact customary law eventually established that anyone who had resided in a city for a year and a day was entitled to this freedom. That is to say people who were dissatisfied with their living conditions and work obligations on estates and in villages subject to feudal lords could become free if they succeeded in absconding from this feudal constraint by moving to towns. Actually in many cases this was a violation of the ban on free movement. But in the highly decentralized and often chaotic situation in rural areas in the Middle Ages, this form of escape was comparatively easy especially for the more adventurous.

Medieval cities were small compared to the much larger urban structures of antiquity. They were also less well equipped with water supply and sanitation facilities. For a long time French kings fought a running battle with the citizens of Paris on the subject of paving the city streets. The king could not simply order them to do it, and it was not until late in the Middle Ages that the condition improved—a situation that sharply outlines the difference in the status of cities in Medieval Europe and in antiquity. But there was the other side of the coin: the freedom of the citizens, and the ever-increasing opportunities to start businesses, to hand them down to descendents over many generations and to start the slow but steady accumulation of capital unhampered by outside power structure. The creation of wealth was predicated in this setting on individual effort and work performance. The foundations were laid for the formation of the middle classes as we know them in the modern world.

One of the great institutions promoting the rise of this class was the guild system. In the declining days of the Roman Empire, Emperor Diocletian had ordered artisans in the cities to form "collegia." All people engaged in the same trade had to join. One of the purposes of this compulsory organization was the attempt to improve the collection of taxes. However, those stern measures could not stem the forces of disintegration in the Roman Empire. One should note that the medieval guilds are not a transfer of this late Roman economic institution into the altogether different setting of the medieval towns.

The guilds started out as voluntary associations of craftsmen and of merchants, with a religious character. In their origins they had aspects of mutual insurance for the purpose of meeting the expenses of a decent burial, masses for the dead, and masses on the feast day of the patron saint of the guild. Soon strictly economic elements were added and eventually the guild system became highly structured and exclusive. As long as cities lacked a full complement of artisans necessary to serve the normal requirements of the local market and as new towns were still being created, the guild system was relatively open. But once in the later Middle Ages this frontier situation no longer prevailed in Europe, the originally free guild system became more and more monopolistic. Yet it was precisely this aspect that facilitated for the happy insiders the acquisition and the accumulation of wealth.

One great achievement of the medieval guilds of craftsmen was the emphasis on skill and performance. Apprenticeship was formalized and no one could rise to the status of journeyman or master who had not completed successfully this first phase, which usually lasted for seven years. Upon graduating to the rank of journeyman the young craftsman was supposed to take to the road and work with masters in other towns. In this way local inbreeding and isolation was overcome, because the system offered opportunities for the exchange of knowledge and the expansion of already acquired skills. After several years of this migratory life, the journeyman was supposed to settle down, present himself for admission to a guild, and demonstrate his ability as a master and thus be accepted as a member.

As time progressed it became more and more difficult for many who started out as apprentices and had become journeymen to make this final step. As the guild system became more rigidly structured, cities would issue charters to local guilds of craftsmen. These proceeded to make entrance requirements more and more difficult. There were in many cases property qualifications. Only people who were freeholders in the city would be admitted as masters. They had to own a house in which they carried on their trade. Practically this established a limit on the number of master craftsmen. Obviously sons or sons-in-law would have an easier time meeting the property requirements than outsiders. Price competition among masters was prohibited in many charters so that the guilds had a monopolistic power over prices charged to the consumer. This was reinforced in many instances by "staple rights"—a system whereby goods transshipped by merchants through cities had to be offered for sale to the local market for a number of days through the intermediacy of the respective local craft guild. In this way the effects of outside competition were minimized.

On the other hand, the guild system provided for the protection of consumers by issuing quality standards to be observed by members of the guild. Customers could make complaints about the quality of products to the overseer of the guild. That this practice continued even in the last part of the eighteenth century is clearly evidenced by Adam Smith's phrase of the "discipline of the market"* which he said was far more effective than the surveyance of quality by guild administrators. While this effect of free competition is undeniably a continuous incentive to improve products and to devise new ones, there is no doubt that the many centuries of guild discipline created in Europe high traditions of workmanship and responsibility conducive not only to the accumulation of capital but also to the formation of a reservoir of skilled labor.

*Wealth of Nations, Chapter 1.

The steady development of the guild system over many centuries of Western Europe led to a gradual build-up of a substantial consumer-goods sector. In many instances consumers could exercise real sovereignty because such important items as furniture, clothing, and shoes were literally made to order according to the specifications of the buyer. Occasionally a family associated with the guild system could acquire great wealth by continuously expanding its activities. This was true, for example of the Fugger family of Augsburg, Germany. Starting out as weavers of expensive materials for clothing they became suppliers of princes and eventually of emperors including Charles V early in the sixteenth century. Very often these highly placed customers were hard pressed for cash and could not pay for deliveries. Eventually the Fuggers were paid off by receiving extensive mining rights especially of silver and quicksilver. They were able to set up a bank which specialized in giving loans to princes. They even advanced funds to Charles V in connection with his election to the office of Emperor by the electoral college of the Old German Reich. When Charles V resigned in 1556 and retired to a monastery in Spain the fortunes of the Fugger bank began to decline and finally that enterprise was liquidated.

The case of the Fugger family is interesting because it represents the transition of master craftsmen to larger-scale economic operations such as mining and banking.

While the independent, middle-class group of medieval artisans were instrumental in developing a large supply of consumer goods long before the start of the factory system and the Industrial Revolution, the medieval merchants and bankers introduced innovations unknown to the Romans, which in the course of time developed into instruments of trade and business techniques that were in wide use when the rate of economic development began to accelerate in Europe in the sixteenth century. Long-distance trade ranging from the Levantine coast of the Eastern Mediterranean through Northern Italy, Southern France, and Southern Germany to Northwestern Europe never ceased completely after the collapse of the Roman economy. Like the artisans, merchants combined in guilds but their activities went beyond the narrow confines of local markets. Early in the Middle Ages trade fairs developed in towns or areas like Lyons, Flanders, and various centers in Germany. The items traded were oriental spices—a great necessity in food preservation in those days—and luxury products such as silks and brocades as well as a variety of wines. Later in the Middle Ages the Leipzig fair became a center of the fur trade. In fact so strong was the tradition created by the medieval trade fairs that these regularly scheduled meetings of large-scale sellers and buyers continue to this day in major European cities, although the emphasis is now on industrial equipment rather than on consumer goods.

Medieval merchants introduced credit buying and forms of business organization that made it possible to expand the size of transactions beyond a primitive barter arrangement or cumbersome cash-and-carry deals. In this way the foundations of substantial accumulations of wealth were laid in Europe during the Middle Ages. The merchants represented in many cities of Northern Europe, an upper class of nonaristocratic origin deriving their wealth not from control over land and labor or from participation in the feudal power structure but from trade and commerce.

Early in the Middle Ages Italian merchants began to use promissory notes. The promise to pay a stated amount of money on the due date—for example six months after the date of issue of the note—was assumed by all signers who put their name on the back of the note. The payee could then ask payment not only from the original debtor but from the others who had assumed the obligation by their endorsement. In this way commercial papers were created making it possible to increase the volume of transaction and expand the scope of business.

Of equal importance was the creation in Northern Italy of the concept and of the practice of the limited liability corporation. While the Romans had introduced such nonpersonal holders of wealth as the "fiscus," public assets of the state as distinct, for instance, from the private property of the emperor, in commercial dealings they only knew the partnership contract. This enabled creditors to collect their claims not only from the share of the partner in the enterprise but also from the totality of his private holdings.

The corporation first developed in connection with the early medieval Levantine trade. Equipping vessels with merchandise for the trip to the Eastern Mediterranean from where they were expected to return with valuable cargoes was a high-risk enterprise. It could bring considerable profits but could also mean a total loss from shipwreck or piracy. In view of this uncertain character medieval merchants began to pool funds for the hiring of a vessel and a captain and for the stocking up of the boats. They would set up a special corporation to carry out this type of trade. The share of the merchants in this corporation would also be the limit of their personal liability. The corporation rather than the individual shareholder became the debtor.

The introduction of the corporate form of business with its limitation of risks encouraged an intensification of trade. When the upsurge of economic growth occurred in Europe toward the end of the Middle Ages, the corporate form of business was fully developed. It was then used for the setting up of such highly profitable, privileged enterprises as the East India Company or the Hudson Bay Company.

Still another breakthrough in business techniques was brought about by the Italian merchants of the Middle Ages. In the fourteenth century a beginning was made with double-entry bookkeeping. Up to that point merchants of antiquity and later times had carefully written down their receipts and their expenditures. These notations, however, left out assets and liabilities such as claims receivable and debts to be paid at some future date. The development of more sophisticated methods of bookkeeping gave additional strength and flexibility to business enterprise.

As the Middle Ages drew to a close, considerable wealth had been accumulated by artisans and especially by merchants in many towns of Europe. Savings began to become substantial. An indication of the availability of funds can be seen in the practice of city governments in the late Middle Ages to sell perpetual rents. These consisted of promises to pay a stated amount of money each year to the holder of such an obligation in return for the payment to the city of the amount of money mentioned in the document. Other indications of wealth accumulation in the late Middle Ages are foundations established by merchants for hospitals and orphanages. The houses of late medieval merchants and artisans also became more spacious and elaborate testifying to the steady increase of wealth of this independent middle class.

The concept of "traditional society" should not be applied to the economic conditions of the economy of medieval Europe. Medieval society is characterized by continuous change and improvements in agricultural, manufacturing and monetary systems. What appears to be a slow moving, tradition-bound period in economic history does so only in the perspective of the age of accelerated growth which did not set in prior to the beginning of the seventeenth century and the first phase of the Industrial Revolution. Another reason for this widespread misinterpretation of economic development of the Middle Ages is based on the fact that in these centuries, predating the start of modern science, the transfer of skills from one generation to the other was carried out in a literal sense by tradition. The accumulated experience in the arts of production of earlier generations was transferred to young workers in the informal setting of the workshops of masters. There was no research carried out along theoretical lines with the objective of improving methods and systems of production. Nevertheless anyone who can observe the transition from the Romanesque to the Gothic style of church architecture in the Middle Ages is aware of the fact that the technology of that age was capable of meeting the complex problems of statics arising from these ambitious building designs. Furthermore, the very history of medieval cathedrals shows that the builders of that age were perfectly willing to abandon the traditional Romanesque style, and in the middle of the long drawn out process of construction change over to an entirely new style, gothic.

It is true, as stressed earlier in this chapter, that throughout this whole period up to the end of the eighteenth century there was no basic change in the labor arrangements either on the feudal estates or in the guild system. Rural labor largely remained unfree, and to a certain extent, bound to the soil. Urban labor within the guild system was rigidly structured along the lines described above. But while these social-economic institutions persisted over long periods of time, the economic operations carried out within this framework underwent considerable changes and improvements. In England in the later Middle Ages big landowners shifted to the large-scale holding of sheep in order to produce a cash crop, wool, which was sold to processors in Flanders and also in England itself. Actually, the peasantry suffered from this commercialization of agriculture because through Enclosure Bills land was withdrawn from common use for pastures of farm livestock and added to the domain of the lord.

While the guild system continued in the cities the number of young men who could not meet the ever-stiffening property requirements and other qualifications of the guilds moved to the suburbs of larger cities where the guild system did not operate. In many cases they were able to set up shops and compete with the established guild masters. Adam Smith referred to this situation in Chapter 10, Part II of his *Wealth of Nations* which appeared in 1776. By that time, however, new economic institutions had come into being which made a powerful contribution to the accumulation of capital.

The *age of discovery* extended the scope of economic operations of Western Europe to the Americas and to the Far East. In Central and Latin America feudalism was introduced and slave labor was added to this type of economic organization. While the plantation system and its slave-labor system was also introduced in North America, there was also a substantial migration of free people from England, Holland, France, Germany, and other countries who settled as independent farmers. Beginning in the seventeenth century, North America was in a position to absorb population pressures developing in Europe, especially in rural areas. However, the incentives for the accumulation of capital as a result of the opening up of the New World were strengthened by the mercantile system.

Mercantilism has been under attack from the very beginning of systematic studies of economics which burst upon the intellectual scene rather suddenly in the middle of the eighteenth century. The criticism of this system voiced by the Physiocrats was valid enough. By that time underlying economic factors of capacity to produce, formation of capital, and rising demand had gained such momentum that such institutions of mercantilism as high protective tariffs, monopolies, and the chartering of corporations with exclusive manufacturing or trading rights began to put brakes on the upsurge of economic development.

However, in the hundred years preceding the voicing of this criticism there had been substantial economic progress and a considerable amassing of wealth under mercantilism. Great privileged trading companies like the East India companies of various countries were set up as joint-stock corporations paying high dividends to shareholders. Profits from the slave trade flowed into Northwestern Europe. Arms manufacturing assumed a larger scale, as did building construction. Wholesale trade developed and jobbers supplied materials to cottage industries especially in textiles. The manufacture of glassware in villages specializing in this trade increased. Water power was used to operate forges in iron works which assumed a size far exceeding the workshops of blacksmiths. Modern, centralized government under absolute monarchies began to require academically trained civil service employees. Learned judges and lawyers were in increasing demand. Universities expanded as scholarship in the humanities and sciences became more diversified. All this led to the formation of a middle class of professional lawyers, professors, and writers thereby adding a new dimension to the old middle-class groups of merchants and artisans.

Banks, originally deposit banks for the clearance of claims between merchants and agents for the collection of taxes, had developed in the Middle Ages. Now the scope of banking activities was extended to commercial banking and investment. Most important, however, was the creation of *central banking* in the period of mercantilism. The Bank of England, which began to operate in 1694, was a typical privileged company of the mercantilistic period. It was conceived as a private corporation and the original stockholders were members of the guild of the goldsmith of London. They deposited gold which they had been holding with the new bank and received an equivalent number of shares in the corporation. Now the privilege granted by the Bank of England centered on the fact that this institution was the bank of issue of bank notes. It had to purchase gold whenever it was offered and against this gold reserve, bank notes could be circulated. The first transaction of the bank consisted in granting a loan to the British government which was secured by the pledging of certain tax revenues. The central bank also would rediscount commercial papers, thereby backing up the whole banking structure. Very soon other European countries followed the example set by the bank of England.

All the developments relating to the accumulation of capital which have been discussed in this section occurred prior to the great acceleration of economic growth which characterizes the last two hundred years. We have seen that even under the guild system a considerable accumulation of wealth was possible, especially as a result of the fact that in many cases the business was held by families for a number of generations and was growing slowly but steadily. The great increase in trade made possible through the setting up of colonies in the Western world with their cash crops of tobacco, sugar, cotton, and coffee afforded additional opportunities for middlemen and whole new layers of middle-class business groups. The expansion of retail trade on the one side, wholesale trade and banking on the other introduced additional opportunities for the growth of wealth through purely economic activities. Eventually the multiplication of these urban business classes decreased the relative economic significance of feudalistic agriculture. In the seventeenth and eighteenth centuries in Western Europe the ruling classes were still the landed nobility. But the urban middle classes, while underrepresented in legislative bodies such as the House of Commons or the Provincial Parliaments in Franch, acquired more and more influence. Long before industrialization gained strength in England and in France, there had occurred an expansion of wealth and of skilled labor and executive manpower.

It is this historical aspect of Western economic development which distinguishes it so markedly from problems of emerging nations as they arise in the period of postcolonialsim late in the twentieth century. If there is one lesson to be learned from economic history for economic development it is that background of the social structure cannot be overlooked in designing models and policies for economic growth. It makes a great difference whether development starts within the context of a labor-accumulation system or whether it can take advantage of a protracted period of capital accumulation which has been outlined in this section. This will be explored further in the next section.

PATTERNS OF ACCUMULATION AND DECISION MAKING

Throughout this chapter we have dealt with historical patterns of accumulation of labor and of capital in order to gain insight into structures of economic development. In the past labor and capital were used in different proportions and combinations and under different social structures to bring about the desired volume of output and of growth in the scope of economic activities. The push outward from already settled areas in the Middle Ages toward new frontiers, gained by clearing forests, draining marshlands, and advancing in a generally Eastern direction in central Europe occurred under feudalism. While the effect of these movements was favorable in economic terms, at no time was there a deliberate, concerted effort to engage in economic development for its own sake. The expansion took place for personal, political, and social reasons rather than for purely economic considerations. Mercantilism was, on the other hand, a set of policies designed to strengthen the efficiency of the economic system through road and canal building, introduction of regular mail and transportation, and the encouragement of industry. For this reason it would be correct to view mercantilism as an economic system dedicated to the proposition that economic development was desirable, that it would not come by itself, and that government had to play an important role in bringing it about. We have already seen in the preceding section that the policies of mercantilism became almost counterproductive in the middle of the eighteenth century. The new science of economics emerging at that time proved that a free competitive market was a far better device for bringing about a general increase in wealth than the rigidly regulated system of the mercantile state.

In the Western world economic theory in general and development theory in particular is still influenced by the triumph of the competitive market model of early economics over mercantilism when the French Revolution set in motion the abolition of all restriction on economic activites. This model preference is still indicated even in the treatment of the novel problems of maintaining the forward, momentum of already highly advanced economic systems in the last decades of the twentieth century. In the twenty-five years since the United States Government in the 1940's began to develop into the largest customer of the private sector and had to allocate ever-increasing amounts of aggregate spending for national defense, space exploration, and research, there had been no significant change in the social assumptions going into macroeconomic models. These profound structural changes of an historical character in the American economy have been treated as almost irrelevant. All this would indicate that there is only an inadequate linkage between the conceptualization of historical transformations of the social economic structure and economic theory proper. These connections, however, exist and they must be brought out in a study of the structure of economic development.

Different forms of accumulation result in different historical patterns of leadership and of decision making. Land-labor accumulation systems usually lead to "ruling classes" with strong tie-ins with high-level military, diplomatic, administrative, and academic leadership groups. Capital-accumulation systems, based on predominantly economic as contrasted to predominantly political forces, lead to the emergence of private entrepreneur, managerial, and professional groups with a great preference to work outside the structure of government and its policies. However, the survival of the "ruling class" type of leadership is not predicated on the formal continuation of feudalism and other labor-accumulation systems. Very often this type of leadership having lost its original economic basis is able to continue its influence by incorporating middle-class groups into its framework. On the other hand, business type leadership continues even in a situation where the main impetus to economic growth comes from government spending. This is often shown in the interchangeability of business and government executives including the Armed Forces so characteristic of the American economy in the 1950's and 1960's. We will now proceed to sketch some predominant characteristics of the decision-making process in the context of a ruling-class background on the one hand and a business-executive basis on the other.

The ruling-class type of leadership groups is more readily found in areas close in time to feudalistic institutions,such as those found in many parts of Latin America but also in England and France. Often educational systems helped to perpetuate this structure. Higher education was "elitist" and only a small number of young people went to colleges and universities. Widespread student unrest reaching a peak in 1968 brought about basic changes in this traditional structure making it more open and flexible.

Most important, formerly colonial countries which retained feudalistic patterns until recently do not have a middle class with a long background of the gradual accumulation of wealth outside the political power structure as it exists in Europe and in the United States. While there is especially in Latin America a high degree of urbanization and a rapid growth of groups engaged in the professions and in business, the scale of priorities in economic development tends to be weighted toward prestige and power symbols. In this respect a certain basic Roman or Latin character reasserts itself in the emphasis being given to monumental structures and plazas utterly different from the simplicity and modesty of early American towns. Generally against this type of background there is a desire to achieve as soon as possible such indicators of success as national airlines and steel mills regardless of whether or not they are justified by a rational economic calculus.

Up until recently young people growing up in such a social setting have shown a great preference for the study of law. There was little emphasis on the study of science, engineering, and business management. We have seen in the preceding chapter that problems of illiteracy still loom very large in developing countries attempting to make a rapid transition from land-accumulation systems to modern industry. On the other hand, in these same countries those who have had some higher education show a good deal of sophistication and are thoroughly grounded in cultural traditions. Just as there is a tendency in these types of systems toward polarization of income distribution between the comparatively few with high earnings and the large masses with extremely limited incomes, there is also very little middle ground in terms of educational achievements. Either they are quite good or they are virtually nonexistent.

The enumeration of these characteristics of leadership groups of countries not too far removed in time from feudalism is not meant as a critique. It is intended to stress that people coming from this background do not speak the same language, even if they use the same words as representatives of nations with a long history of the gradual evolution of a middle class and a market and consumer-oriented system. The recent feudalistic background coupled with a high-level liberal arts education very often induces a verbal approach, an acceptance of paper solutions and of a wide gap between actual developments and proclaimed economic and social objectives. Furthermore, they will be inclined to think more in terms of government regulation and intervention and will tend to prefer a mixed-economy model of development policy.

Businessmen, government officials, and negotiators from countries with a long-established middle-class pattern have an entirely different frame of reference. They are inclined to view economic development as a result of individual effort, of the rational use of limited means with an objective of maximizing returns and profits. For this reason growth targets and development goals are viewed very often in a purely economic context. Furthermore, recent adoption of more democratic political institutions by developing countries is all too often equated with a real transformation of the traditional social structure and a liquidation of the psychological thought and behavior patterns connected with them. Occasionally there is often an unconscious assumption made by men with middle-class backgrounds that people from underveloped countries are of somewhat inferior intelligence. It is obvious that an encounter between representatives of these two groups—one coming from a labor-accumulation system and another from a capital accumulation structure—

is bound to lead to many misunderstandings and faulty designs of development schemes.

The foregoing discussion has hinted at the great weight that historical circumstances have in economic development. However, there are other basic structures of the dynamics of economic growth of a more general nature which also must be taken into account. We will now turn to them.

chapter **3**

Systematic Aspects of
Economic Development

The brief overview of economic development presented in Chapter 1 revealed that for the greater part of history the rate of growth of the economic system was extremely slow. It is only in recent centuries that a great speed-up of economic development has occurred. As we approach the end of the twentieth century a further acceleration of this trend has set in. This condition is due to two entirely different configurations of development. They must be kept clearly distinct for purposes of analysis and for the shaping of policies for economic development.

For a large part of the globe where the majority of the world population is located and where population pressures are most intense, acceleration of development is posited by the rapid growth in numbers of people requiring more food, more housing, more education, more transportation and more employment opportunities. In the more advanced areas of the world rates of population growth have started to decline sharply from post-World War II levels. However, in these areas the transformation of the labor force brought about by advanced technology and automation imposes on these highly developed economic systems the need to accelerate the rate of growth even further in order to avoid serious internal and external economic and social imbalances. Given the exceedingly rapid pace of technological change, there is no terminal point of economic development in sight even for complex or advanced systems. The whole problem of economic development is, therefore, not only of relevance to so-called underdeveloped or emerging nations but also of social significance for areas and countries which by all acceptable criteria are leaders in economic advance.

One of the pitfalls in economic development policy is the application of development patterns of highly advanced countries to those areas which need economic development very urgently but have only recently emerged from feudalistic structures or are still characterized by large scale tribal village subsistence sectors. While the temptation is very great in these emerging nations to engage in "great leaps forward," such ambitions are apt to distort the proper allocation of manpower and resources without which the economic development will not succeed. Industrialization and urbanization becomes inevitable as a result of the transition from primitive agricultural conditions to that type of diversification of the economic structure which is made necessary by population pressures and technical progress. But unless basic improvements can be achieved first for the vast masses of a rural population, the modern sector of the economy, the towns and factories will remain mere window dressing, like the so-called "Potemkin villages" surrounded by an economic wasteland.

The great technical advances in agriculture, industry, construction, transportation, and communication have made available a great variety of systems and patterns which can be adopted for the purpose of designing and carrying out development targets and plans. In this unprecedented situation there is great pressure to use indiscriminately advanced techniques merely because they are available. However, this transfer of methods that have been working in developed countries to areas with different historical and social structures can lead to waste, frustration and even counterproductive effects.

SCENARIOS OF DEVELOPMENT SITUATIONS

An approach to economic development informed by insights into the significance of historical conditions must attempt to set up classifications of development situations. Only by making distinctions of this type will it be possible to select appropriate development models. It should be noted that this type of analysis must precede any attempts at computerizing and working out specific techniques and policies of economic development.

The common denominator of all types of economic development is increase and diversification of output. Given the great emphasis on formation and accumulation of capital in the development of industrial countries, it is easy to see why most approaches to economic development stress the factor capital and the strategic role of savings and investments in the promotion of economic growth. However, on a more general level, taking into account the vast disparities in the stages of economic development throughout the world from tribal village to highly industrialized systems, it is necessary to keep in view not only capital but also labor as a factor in development. The proper design of factor proportions implies decisions not only about the rate of build-up of social overhead capital, heavy and light industries and agricultural resources and output, but also about the mix of the labor and capital factors themselves. Today there are vast areas in which economic development is retarded but where labor supply is abundant. The more efficient and productive use of labor is an important aspect of economic development in nations starting on the path to economic development. This factor use will not lead to high rates of growth but it is likely to insure a more balanced spread of progress over all differentiating and evolving sectors of the economy.

Clearly then a choice must be made in the design of economic development between maximum and optimum goals over a given period of time. Political considerations may induce leadership groups to embark on maximum speed developments. This certainly was the road selected in the Soviet Union under Stalin prior to World War II when the Communists were fearful of "capitalistic encirclement." To achieve spectacular annual growth rates is usually a goal formulated within a political rather than an economic context. Optimum growth tries to combine annual advances in the output and productivity of the system with a more even spread of development to all sectors of the economy and the labor market.

It would be too narrow to view output maximization as the sole criterion of economic growth and development. Especially with the availability of advanced production methods and systems, increases in agricultural and industrial output can be achieved while labor requirements decline. What appears as a feasible economic maximum output goal may be inconsistent with the social goal of preventing technological labor displacements in the former subsistence sector.

A reconsideration of increased output goals and employment targets is an essential aspect of development design. The proper timing of labor force restructuring is necessary to prevent a further rise of favelas and shanty towns at the periphery of mushrooming metropolitan areas.

Actually economic development can be brought about by *factor multiplication* or by *factor transformation.* Concretely there will be in most cases a combination of these two methods.

Factor multiplication takes place when gradually more units, especially additional land and additional labor, are being put into use while the technique of production itself remains basically the same. During the Middle Ages this was the way in which an internal frontier was gradually reached in European countries through the draining of swamps in river valleys and the clearing of primeval forests. Such projects increased total output and employment and eventually brought the system to a higher stage of development without the introduction of radical innovations in production methods.

Factor transformation takes place when a substitution occurs between various sources of energy—for instance, the replacement of human and animal muscle power by mechanical energy such as water, steam, and electricity. Industrialization will lead to more rapidly rising rates of growth than is possible under factor multiplication.

In emerging countries, output and employment optima can be reached by labor-intensive methods even at the cost of not utilizing all technologically feasible production methods. In more advanced countries in which the process of diversification has already taken root and where new industries, lines of consumer goods, and types of services are being developed, output maximization will be able to proceed while fully taking advantage of increases in output per man-hour, corresponding decreases in unit labor requirements, and the rise of employment opportunities in the nonproduction sector. However, in the most advanced countries such as the United States there comes eventually a point in economic development when the concern for optimum levels of employment reappears and when a new balance is being worked out between output and employment targets.

We can demonstrate the changing relations between output and employment goals with a general curve depicting output-employment ratios. This curve will show different slopes in the map which covers three main Phases of economic development:

Early development (ED)
Accelerated development (AD)
Development beyond affluence (DBA)

Early development is characterized by factor multiplication, especially more intensive use of the factor labor. *Accelerated development* is characterized by the ever-increasing use of capital and the substitution of mechanical energy for human labor. Eventually a high degree of mechanization and automation is reached. As output increases unit labor requirements decline. More and more can be produced without an increase in the number of production workers. Finally a stage is reached in advanced countries in which nonproduction workers begin to outnumber at an ever greater degree manual workers in industry, agriculture, and transportation. Yet even such systems must continue to grow in order to accommodate a further increase in the labor force and rising demand for employment. When development must continue *beyond affluence* labor requirements will begin to rise. But this time the increase will be on the managerial, professional, and supervisory level and in white-collar employment in general.

On the figure shown here the vertical axis represents levels of output and/or income, the horizontal axis shows numbers of workers. The line *E-E* indicates output employment ratios characteristic of the three phases of economic development shown.

Output-Employment Ratios in Various Stages
of Economic Development

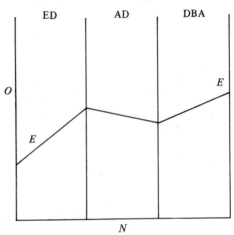

The output-employment pattern in developing countries just emerging from simple and primitive conditions indicates that growth is generated by the increasing use of all factors. That is to say factor multiplication is the prevailing pattern of development. The increase in output is due primarily to an expansion of already existing production patterns and systems. This we have called development by *factor multiplication*.

Accelerated growth is indicative of *factor transformation*. Under this process capital is increasingly substituted for labor and generally speaking output increases much faster than employment. In extreme cases of factor transformation such as in American agriculture, output rises sharply as employment declines at a rapid rate. Under such circumstances aggregate levels of optimum employment can be maintained only if there is a compensatory expansion of nonproduction employment and generally speaking a transition from a blue-collar to a white-collar economy.

There are, however, limits to this type of labor force transformation. Pockets of persistent unemployment remain which become costly and contribute to new social and economic imbalances in mature economic systems. It is at this point that a new concern develops to find a middle way between optimum output and employment targets. In the 1960's first attempts were made in the United States to deal with this problem by inducing changes in the concept of employability and creating incentives for the absorption of chronically unemployed into the active labor force. Admittedly these are novel problems which come into sight only as an economy has reached extremely high levels of productivity, diversification, and output.

Choices between maximum and optimum levels of output and of employment are only the most general aspect of development patterns. We will now proceed to outline five different basic situations or *scenarios* of economic development. In gathering data for specific development designs, it is necessary to decide first into which of these five basic structures a concrete development situation fits best. These basic situations can be stated as follows:

A. Early Development (ED)

1. Increase in output and employment through increased use of given factors without change in factor proportions.
2. Balanced growth through simultaneous investment in the producer goods, consumer and public sectors while factor proportions change in favor of capital.

B. Accelerated Development (AD)

3. Deliberately unbalanced growth by priority investment in heavy industry and social overhead capital.
4. Maintenance of balanced growth of real income by protecting factor shares against inflationary potential in AD situations.

C. Growth Beyond Affluence (GBA)

5. Change from output maximization goals to a concern for optimum relations between rates of change in output, in employment and income shares.

These five scenarios of economic development are related to different historical points of departure of economic growth. We will briefly outline these typical situations.

Scenario 1. This situation applies to all processes of expansion which require additional inputs of capital and of labor under the sectoral-growth pattern. That is to say while output increases, this development will also bring about a proportionate increase in employment. In this situation there is no contradiction between maximum goals of output on the one side and desired maxima of employment on the other. As factor input increases so will aggregate factor payments. This is a scenario in which Say's law seems to be operative. In this case it is being assumed that there is no change in technology and in output per man hour. This development model does not provide for factor transformation, merely for an across the board increase in factor utilization. This scenario still fits into problems of emergent countries where there is an increasing imbalance between population and agricultural output. More land must be worked by more people in the initial stages of this type of development.

Scenario 2. This setting represents the basic structure of development in most countries of Western Europe. Long before the first industrial revolution got under way, the consumer sector was large and diversified. Trade was international; and social overhead capital in form of roads, canals, postal systems, and higher education was being created beginning with the sixteenth century. When technological advances brought about the replacement of human and animal energy by mechanical energy resources the rate of investment through the creation of new industries and transportation systems increased sharply. However, in this model there was no need to repress or retard the expansion of the consumer sector. Hence in this scenario balanced growth resulted without the imposition of priorities on the one side and restraints on the other. In this case there was considerable factor transformation. As productivity increased labor requirements per output declined. But through the successive introduction of new industries—textile, railroads, iron and steel, metals, electric, automotive, chemical—there was such an overall rate of expansion that aggregate demand for labor increased, thereby compensating for the decrease in unit labor requirements. In this scenario, the free-factor market of labor and capital operated with a high degree of efficiency for the simple reason that prior to the start of industrialization there had been accumulated vast resources of skilled manpower. Efficient public administration had been established. At the beginning of this development there was no proportionate sharing in the gains of this progressive situation. However, over the course of about three generations labor was able to benefit increasingly from this capital accumulation system by obtaining substantial wage boosts and fringe benefits. It must be realized that this capitalistic scenario is determined by its specific historical background and the timing of the start of accelerated development. A transfer of this scenario to entirely different historical and social conditions cannot produce similar favorable results.

Scenario 3. This unbalanced-growth model indicates an underlying situation of great urgency. Such a permanent crisis condition can have entirely different causes. The common denominator, however, is that there is at the point of departure an all pervasive condition of relative or absolute scarcity of existing resources and that development goals can only be reached by accelerating the build-up of one sector at the expense of restraining others. This was the situation at the start of the Communist system in the Soviet Union. There had occurred a real breakdown in the operations—production, transportation, and public services—of the old system. Superimposed on this crisis situation was the desire of the Communists to create in a short period of time a modern industrial system for which the preconditions in terms of manpower and capital resources which are part of Scenario 2 were not immediately available. There emerged a system of rigidly enforced priorities on the build-up of heavy industries including armaments and on public utilities and transportation. The rate of growth of the consumer goods and of the agricultural product sector was deliberately retarded. Unlike the balanced-growth model of economic development this entailed a great deal of deprivation not only for the rapidly increasing class of industrial workers but also for the rural population and especially for the relatively small group of former property owners. It should be noted that Scenario 3 looks entirely different depending on the social history and location of the observer. If such a person belongs to formerly privileged groups the scene appears completely black and desolate. If looked at from the perspective of those who never had any material or educational advantages, bright spots may be visible.

Unbalanced growth is, however, not necessarily identified with Communist patterns of economic development. The great urgency which forces the setting up of priorities in growth targets can also be brought about by population pressures, especially if they are permitted to spill over from the rural areas to rapidly growing and partly deteriorating urban centers. Here priorities may be indicated for the rapid building up of industrial employment opportunities, for the expansion of output of import substitutes and on construction. This cannot be achieved with Scenario 2 market structures and will require channeling of investment, incentives to capital formation, and restraints on consumer income.

Scenario 4. This situation refers to the frequent case that economic development is accompanied by strong inflationary pressures. If they become overpowering there may be a cessation of real growth of the economy. Eventually this inflation scenario can lead to negative economic development or to stagnation. Once such a situation has become chronic it can be remedied only by most radical measures such as the withdrawal of the old currency and its replacement with a new one. However, the stability of the new currency is predicated on the ability of the system to bring about a balanced increase in real-income shares. Otherwise the inflationary spiral will start again.

Scenario 5. This situation can only occur after a protracted period of economic growth, a sharp rise in output and in labor productivity. In such a technologically advanced situation the problem of maintaining full employment becomes more difficult especially if this scenario is displaying a nonwar setting. At this point output goals and production systems must be fitted into optimum goals and production methods must be adjusted into optimum goals of employment in order to prevent the scenario from splitting up into a dual structure with prosperity in the center and poverty on all sides.

Scenarios 1 and 2 cover the greater part of the history of economic development. Present problems of economic development are represented in Scenario 3 as far as most centrally planned economies are concerned and also in those vast areas which are under particularly strong population pressures. The latter group of situations is also involved in Scenario 4 while very advanced nations such as the United States are beginning to move into Scenario 5.

It has been suggested at the beginning of this chapter that the mere availability of modern technology does not necessarily justify their immediate application especially in emergent countries in which output and employment optima must be sought simultaneously. Hence even today Scenario 1 has great significance. It is characterized by sectoral growth of given factors. For this reason this growth pattern as well as the case of factor transformation will now be taken up in somewhat greater detail.

SECTORAL GROWTH OF FACTORS

The most important aspect of sectoral growth is the increase in land utilization. In very primitive conditions this can occur through the burning over of brushland and converting it to agricultural uses. It can also assume the form of clearings in primeval forests. Frequently marshlands in plains and river valleys have been drained to increase land utilization. Another very early method of increasing land use was the establishment of irrigation systems, such as in ancient Egypt and in the Near East empires of antiquity. Very early in the history of the Phoenicians and Greeks there was an insufficiency of arable land to serve the increasing agricultural needs of a growing population. These nations resorted to colonization around the fringes of the Mediterranean in order to gain additional land. In the case of the Phoenicians this land was used for the setting up of a plantation type of agriculture utilizing native slave labor. For the Greeks, colonies served as an outlet for a relative surplus population for which the domestic factor land had run out. Land use was extended in the Roman Empire through the distribution of agricultural land to veterans of the Roman Legion especially in the rich area of what is today Romania. Until the thirteenth century there was still free land available in continental European countries which could be put to use by pioneer farmers, often younger sons of feudal lords moving to the frontier with younger sons of tenant farmers. The westward move of Americans in the nineteenth century, strengthened by the Homestead Act of 1861, is a more recent example of sectoral growth by increasing the agricultural area under cultivation.

Sectoral expansion is not confined to developing countries. It is going on vigorously in the last third of the twentieth century in the Netherlands, one of the most developed countries in the Western world. Ever since World War I draining projects have been going on to convert the huge water inlet of the North Sea—the Zuider Zee—into arable land. Already 302,000 acres have been reclaimed and when the project is completed around 1990 the land area of Holland will have been increased by 7 percent. A new province will have been created and a new city, Lelystad, is already under construction. The purpose of this plan is to create additional farms, relieve fairly strong population pressures and to reduce urban congestion in the existing metropolitan areas of Holland. The opening up of virgin land areas in Western Siberia in the 1950's is another example of sectoral growth. This project, beset by many difficulties—partly due to unfavorable conditions of climate, partly to administrative inefficiency—was intended to increase the total factor land in the agricultural sector of the Soviet economy.

Throughout history the main instrumentality of bringing about a sectoral growth was the availability of labor. In New England farms as distinct from plantations using slave labor, were developed by free labor. In the early colonial days of Virginia, contracts of indenture between farm owners and young men coming from England, binding them to their master for seven years offered the very important bonus that at the expiration of the term of service, the young men were entitled to receive free land for the development of his own farm. This form of labor contract became less frequent toward the end of the seventeenth century. But while it was in use, it made opportunities available for young people which were completely absent in the British Isles at that time.

Extension of agricultural areas, especially in form of the settlement of hitherto unpopulated areas inevitably brings about processes of growth in nonagricultural occupations. Small scale production of consumer goods and of simple agricultural equipment will be carried out in villages and small towns. In this way the original growth of the factor land will lead as it were in the second round to an expansion of capital. If these processes of growth can continue over a number of generations, as they have been in many instances throughout history, this will lead to a slow but steady increase in output and in wealth.

The "frontier" was reached in Europe in the fourteenth century; in the United States the westward expansion of farming and a general frontier situation came to an end about the turn of the nineteenth century. There are vast internal frontiers even today in such countries as Brazil and Venezuela, in certain parts of China and even the Soviet Union. Potentially expansion and diversification of agriculture is a sectoral growth pattern available in many parts of Africa.

At this point in our study of sectoral growth it must be remembered that the historical illustrations and even the outline of future possibilities of this type of economic development are concerned with situations in which existing technology of land use is being applied for the opening up of new areas. That is to say this type of growth is labor-intensive. It does not provide for a spectacular increase of agricultural output per acre or per man hour but rather for a rise in aggregate production. In the first round of this development such sectoral growth might be designed to maintain a balance between population pressures against agricultural resources and the total output of these productive assets. This model of economic development would require, as it always has in the past, some social overhead capital in terms of road building, setting up of transportation systems, storage facilities, schools and dispensaries. Such labor intensive growth processes, shunning the utilization of the most advanced equipment would seem to be preferable to accelerated modernization of hitherto backward areas because the latter method is bound to result in one of the most serious paradoxes of development: displacement of rural populations by the introduction of industrialized agriculture, the flight of rural people to shanty towns around urban centers and the transformation of rural underemployment into urban structural unemployment. This problem is discussed in greater detail in Chapter 4.

Sectoral growth of land use in emerging nations meets formidable obstacles in areas where as a result of former feudalistic or slave economy types of land and labor accumulation, great disproportionalities continue in the distribution of land ownership. This is particularly true of many areas in Central and South America. Very often modest beginnings in redistribution of land such as have occurred in Chile and in Columbia are strongly resisted by still powerful "oligarchies." In Guatemala, where 2 percent of the farm operators control 80 percent of the agricultural area, even most modest reforms were successfully resisted by the big landowners in the late 1960's. Land reform is not a panacea for underdevelopment and underemployment. Occasionally such schemes have been attempted without proper preparation. They cannot succeed without a minimum outlay of social overhead capital and educational efforts to improve the skill of the rural population. On the other hand, successful resistance to land reform even in the form of attempts to make hasty transitions from feudalistic to industrialized methods of land utilization, can only aggravate the basic situation characterized by a rapidly rising population on the one side and a shortage of productive employment opportunities on the other.

Ultimately technological progress cannot be forestalled. However, in underdeveloped and overpopulated areas sectoral growth should be the development pattern of choice. It should precede by at least one generation the other type of economic development, factor transformation. Actually, sectoral growth is the middle way, and in many cases the only rational way of avoiding continuation of economic primitivism or a relapse into it behind a façade of superficial economic progress in the form of mere window dressing. This, however, seems to be the danger in such areas as the former Belgian Congo, Nigeria, and Kenya.

It was stressed at the beginning of this section that for the purposes of analysis it is advisable to keep processes of sectoral growth quite distinct from development through factor transformation. This procedure has helped us understand the desirability of the sectoral-growth patterns in many areas in which population pressures are becoming more acute year after year. In actuality, sectoral growth will not only have to use existing technology but will also be able to take advantage of some aspects of innovations and inprovements. This would refer especially to crop protection through insecticides, crop improvement through fertilizers, and crop diversification. But at this early phase it would preclude introduction of large-scale motorized and mechanized farm equipment which presupposes vast areas and large sizes in agricultural units.

More important is the extension of training in more effective methods of farming, such as better soil utilization and conservation, use of better breeds of plants, and improved marketing techniques. Hand in hand with this specialized educational effort, rural schools must be expanded and health stations introduced. The latter are of direct economic impact. In many underdeveloped parts of the world, work efficiency is low not only as a result of poor nutrition but also because many people are suffering from chronic debilitating diseases which impair work performance and motivation.

Only after these basic improvements have taken root does it make sense to comtemplate more mechanized systems of farming in these areas. Even then it will be necessary to find a proper balance between output targets and employment goals. Overall optimum social and economic considerations must have preference over specialized maximum levels of production.

This emphasis on optimum output-employment ratios does not preclude the creation of an "industrialized" farm sector dedicated to the mass production of such items as bananas, pineapples, citrus fruits, and similar items provided that these units do not displace smaller farms but are an addition to the total output.

Wherever agricultural activities can expand along the lines of a sectoral-growth model unencumbered by the intrusion of exigencies of factor transformation, total output and productivity will rise slowly. But the cumulative effect of such a steady advance will benefit the system as a whole. A study of agricultural developments preceding the acceleration of growth brought about by the Industrial Revolution in Europe makes this point very clear. As has been shown by E. L. Jones*, the increasing use of new plants such as clover and turnips led to an increase in fodder crops and eventually to a substantial augmentation of livestock. All this did not require great changes in farm implements. One interesting by-product of this more intensive system of farming was a substantial drop in grain prices.*

There is no reason to assume that in the twentieth century sectoral-growth patterns in agriculture enabling more people to engage in agriculture in newly opened up areas of emerging countries is no longer feasible. The great advances in technology should be applied rather judiciously in these areas. Emphasis should be placed on diversification, improved seeds and methods of fertilization rather than on mechanization. A mix of labor

*See the two papers by E. L. Jones, "Agricultural Productivity and Economic Growth 1700-1760," and "Agriculture and Economic Growth in England 1660-1750," *Journal of Economic History,* Vol. XXV (March 1965).

intensive methods and nonmachine aspects of innovations in agricultural production is apt to increase output of food rather rapidly while providing employment opportunities for the growing population outside of urban centers with their high rates of unemployment.

Sectoral growth is not confined to agriculture. It can also be promoted in the capital sector through the encouragement of light industries primarily for the production of consumer goods items hitherto unknown or scarce in underdeveloped rural areas. In fact, even in the highly industralized Soviet Union, a go-ahead signal was given to collective farmers in 1967 to set up cooperative, small-scale production units to satisfy such local or regional needs. This was done in order to increase year-round employment opportunities in rural areas of the Soviet Union, to create incentives for younger people to stay on the farm, and to supplement the output of mass-production consumer-goods industries.

This type of economic development can progress best with Scenario 1 outlined above. Increase in output must be combined with high rural employment goals. This must continue until such time that the growth in other sectors of the economy can provide additional employment opportunities. A balanced growth of the agricultural sector both in terms of output, employment, and income must be the first phase in the chain of development from primitive to more modern systems of the rural economy. Proper timing is essential in order to avoid huge dislocations of people, their uprooting in rural areas, and the transfer of rural destitution to rapidly developing urban and shanty town slums in the centers and on fringes of large cities.

This smooth transition stretched out over an appropriate period of time can be achieved only if there is a slow phasing-in of a new technology rather than a sudden transition from primitivism to supertechnology. To achieve tremendous increases in output in a short period at the expense of large-scale labor displacement may yield economic gains of a rather illusory character. In many parts of the world, including the United States, large numbers of people displaced by the agricultural revolution have sought refuge in urban conglomorates. The great strides in cost effectiveness of production are increasingly being upset by the rapidly growing ineffectiveness of local administration and their inability to keep financially abreast of the rising money requirements caused by this transition.

The discussion in this section has shown the need to exercise a certain freedom of choice between the two basic types of economic development. Sectoral growth which was the predominant pattern of economic development throughout most of economic history cannot be ruled out as a valid and workable method for the future. The proper mix between capital and labor in investment designed to promote development remains one of the most important issues in policy models. In order to analyze this further we will now pay closer attention to the second type of economic development: factor transformation. It is characteristic of all advanced industrial countries but most of all the United States. We will demonstrate some aspects of this pattern of development by referring to transformations within the American economy.

FACTOR TRANSFORMATION

We have stressed that for the greater part of economic history development to higher levels of output was predicated on an increase in the use of land and labor factors. Even in the first phase of capitalism in the seventeenth century, usually referred to as merchant capitalism and mercantilism, the additions to capital were mostly in the form of ships inventories or increases in the volume of transactions through dealing in new staple crops such as sugar, tobacco, tea, and coffee. Labor remained the main factor of production in this first stage of the capitalistic system. Gradually the number of nonproduction workers increased in the offices of bankers, traders, and shopkeepers. However, the size of enterprise remained small for a considerable period and the bulk of the population continued to work in agriculture and in strictly manual occupations. This structure underwent decisive changes in the course of the three revolutions through which economic development has been moving at an ever-accelerating rate.

Up until recently the replacement of much of human and animal energy through the steam engine, electric power, and the gasoline motor has been called the Industrial Revolution. From the vantage point of the late twentieth century we can see now that this was only the *first* Industrial Revolution. It was followed in the twentieth century by an *agricultural* revolution. After World War II automation and other great strides in science and industrial technology have inaugurated the *second* Industrial Revolution.

These three revolutions, unlike sectoral growth processes, have brought about far-reaching transformations of the factors of production. Such changes do not only apply to the capitallabor ratio—they also affect the factor management. The second Industrial Revolution has changed the nature of entrepreneurship. We will discuss the transformation of the capital labor ratio as well as of the managerial factor in this section. In this analysis we will refer to developments in the United States because it is here that transformations have gone further than anywhere else.

The radical transformation of the factor labor can be seen clearly in the restructuring of the labor force of the United States in the last hundred years. The table on page 80 supplies this information.

This table shows clearly the revolutionary changes in the agricultural sector of the American economy. Farm employment in 1929 still was 12.7 million; in 1965, it had dropped to 6.4 million. While farm employment was virtually cut in half within one generation, farm output almost doubled. On the basis of 1957–59 = 100, total farm output in 1929 was 62 and in 1965, 115. The most striking advances in productivity of labor measured in output per man hour were not made in industry. They occurred in agriculture. Output per man hour in farming was almost 40 percent higher in 1965 than it had been in 1960.

A hundred years ago the United States had just ceased to be a predominantly agricultural country. Manufacturing already claimed a sizable proportion—17.6 percent of the total labor force. The increase in the relative share of employment in manufacturing, 25.9 percent in 1965, is far less of a change than the dramatic drop of employment in agriculture. In 1965 an all-time high in manufacturing employment was reached when for the first time it exceeded 18 million. A previous peak had occurred in 1953 when employment stood at 17.5 million. But while employment in manufacturing between 1953 and 1965 rose by less than 5 percent, output in manufacturing increased by more than 50 percent. This means that due to continued improvements in production systems this quantum jump in production could be achieved with a very small increase in total employment in manufacturing. But these overall figures do not reveal the full extent of the factor transformation in the American economy. No distinction has been made so far between manual, production workers in manufacturing and clerical or nonproduction workers associated with the industries. In 1953 already 19.9 percent of the employees in manufacturing belonged to the clerical worker category; in 1965 this ratio had risen to 25.6 percent.* If we take this into account we discover that actually only 13.4 million production workers were needed in 1965 against more than 14 million in 1953. Production worker output per man hour, therefore, increased at a rate of more than 4 percent per annum in this period.

Here we encounter one of the main characteristics of factor transformation: in a *technologically progressive system changes in output and*

*See *Manpower Report of the President,* April 1967, Table C-5.

Percentage Distribution of Employed Labor Force in the United States 1869–1965*

Year or Period	Agriculture	Mining	Contract Construction	Manufac- turing	Transporta- tion and Communica- tion & Pub- lic Utilities	Trade and Finance	Services	Government
1869	48.3	1.3	4.9	17.6	5.1	8.2	11.1	3.5
1899	36.9	2.5	4.9	20.0	7.7	12.0	11.9	4.1
1919	24.6	2.7	3.6	25.1	9.4	15.3	10.7	8.6
1929	19.9	2.2	5.0	22.8	8.8	20.3	14.0	6.9
1948– 53	10.6	1.6	5.6	26.7	6.9	21.5	13.1	13.9
1965	5.7	.9	5.6	25.9	5.6	22.7	16.5	17.0

*Adapted from *Long-Term Economic Growth, 1860–1965*, U.S. Department of Commerce.

changes in employment of production workers move in opposite directions. More can be produced while fewer people are being employed. However, the table presented above and the analysis given in the preceding paragraph show that at least for the time being a rapidly progressing but already fully developed system has created offsets to technological labor displacement through a rapid increase in nonproduction types of employment. This is true, as we have seen, of manufacturing industries themselves. It is also indicated in the steady growth of employment in the private sector in such areas as trade and finance and in services. Furthermore, government has become a major source of employment. Whereas in 1869 only 3.5 percent of the labor force was employed in the public sector, the proportion had risen to 17 percent in 1965. Actually in that year almost as many people were in that segment of the labor force than had been in manufacturing almost one hundred years earlier.

The United States is the most advanced country and is, therefore, a prototype of development of advanced countries undergoing accelerated processes of factor transformation. The experience in the United States seemed to indicate a pattern which must assert itself elsewhere whenever this American type of economic development becomes feasible due to technological advances and the utilization of the economics of scale as it has become possible for instance through the establishment of the European Common Market. These patterns are:

1. Increases in agricultural and industrial output become associated with an actual decline in production workers.
2. A general transformation of the labor force occurs through a shift from production to nonproduction types of employment.
3. Continued full employment of an advanced system is predicated on the creation of new employment opportunities in trade, finance, insurance, services, the professions, education and government.
4. The transformation of factors and the shift to nonproduction employment requires a radical upgrading of educational and occupational standards of the labor force.
5. In order to sustain rates of private and public spending commensorate with ever-increasing output potentials, the growth rate of highly developed systems far from slowing down must continue to accelerate.

The discussion of economic development characterized by rapid factor transformation, spreading technology and proliferation of nonproduction activities shows that this type of expansion is structurally different from development patterns predicated on sectoral growth. Unless these two types of economic development are kept clearly separate, the inevitable failures caused by the application of the wrong model are bound to accentuate even further the still-widening gap between the levels of output and standards of living of advanced and developing areas of the globe. Inasmuch as population pressures are increasing far more rapidly in underdeveloped countries, misinterpretations of the historical setting in these countries, and miscalculations in the design and sequence of development plans are bound to contribute to a further aggravation of this international disequilibrium.

It was already stated that factor transformation changing in a radical way the capital-labor ratio and the proportion between production and nonproduction employment have profound effects on the way in which the factor management is operated. This requires further investigation.

DECISION MAKING IN ECONOMIC DEVELOPMENT

The conventional model of a market economy assumes that decision making is located in the private sector of the economy. It can be measured in terms of an increase in private investment, especially for additional plant and equipment and residential construction. Private-investment decisions are brought about by expectations of profits. These in turn are shaped by assumed increases in consumer spending, market responses to new products and the ability to raise profits through favorable cost-price ratios. In conformity with this model, economic development is seen as the almost unintended result of a large number of private investment decisions all made within the frame of reference just outlined. Public spending and government intervention are assumed to be relatively insignificant compared to overall expenditures in the consumer and in the business sector of the gross national product (GNP). The role of government is often seen primarily as a custodian of the institutions of a free-market economy. It follows that the creation of a climate favorable to private investment was considered one of the most important contributions that government could make in the promotion of economic growth.

This model assumes that investment decisions are made in the private sector by a considerable number of firms in particular industries. It implies that there has not been any substantial concentration in very large firms, absorbing smaller ones and changing a predominantly free competitive market system into one in which competition is imperfect or monopolistic. In spite of the divergence of actual economic structures from this model in many directions, such as far greater involvement of government through large-scale public spending, or the domination of the market by large business concerns, there are some instances of rather rapid economic development which actually were initiated primarily by the creation of a favorable climate for investment.

An outstanding example of such a situation would be the "bootstrap" system of encouraging economic development in Puerto Rico. The government of that island has offered substantial tax advantages to business concerns deciding to locate there or to open new branches. In this way private investment was attracted because due to favorable production costs profits expectations were high. Actually the availability of tax savings, often combined with lower local labor cost, can operate even today as a significant incentive in the private investment sector of developing countries.

It is important, however, to view such developments in the context of the profound change in business operations and in the factor of management itself. Investment in foreign ventures involving high risks on the one side but also the possibility of making high profits on the other, was one of the first aspects of merchant capitalism. "Venture capital" was put into such privileged companies as the Virginia, Hudson Bay, East India, and similar companies. The early eighteenth-century French Mississippi Company which ended in the notorious "Mississippi Bubble" of 1722 is another illustration of the highly speculative character of such daring and sometimes disastrous private enterprises. The information available in this early capitalistic type of decision making and investment was often not only incomplete but outright wrong. Some of these commercial ventures succeeded in spite of the misinformation and wrong expectations that led to their creation in the first place. Others like the Mississippi Company failed completely.

The rapid economic growth of the United States, Canada, Australia, and other parts of former empire and colonial structures in the nineteenth century was promoted to a considerable extent be an overflow of European capital to the rest of the world. Prior to World War I the United States was not engaged in large-scale foreign investment. It was still absorbed primarily in the unprecedented build-up of its own industrial system, which by that time had become the strongest in the world. But throughout this period of steady advance, the import of foreign capital as well as immigrant labor was a prerequisite for maintaining the forward momentum of the economy. Throughout this protracted period of growth

European capitalists showed a great preference for foreign investment. Domestically priority was given to investments in export industries and the consumer sector was kept below its full potential. The emphasis on foreign investment and on exports kept growth rates of European economies within certain bounds although the upward push was steady and accelerating, especially in the twenty years preceding World War I.

Compared to the merchant adventurers of an early age, the European investor in foreign economic development was more prudent and better advised. Private investment bankers did play a prominent role in channeling capital from Europe to other parts of the world. The impact of the first Industrial Revolution made investments more rational and secure than they had been in the earlier period in which speculation and the hope to get rich quick provided more emotional motivations. Now this type of international flow of capital into developing areas was predicated on two important facts. First, in the receiving countries there existed a class of resourceful and efficient managers. Secondly, this investment in developing countries was carried out through the purchase of stocks and bonds in corporations set up in these nations. It did not take place in the form of establishing subsidiaries of domestic companies or the purchase of already existing business enterprises. In this way the influx of capital into developing areas did not distort to any degree the competitive character of the system and was not of itself a cause for the transformation of the market structure into a monopolistic system. Development decisions originated in the private sector in the country that was making capital available as well as in receiving nations.

This type of decision making in economic development has become the exception under the conditions prevailing toward the end of the twentieth century. There are several causes for this change. The first set of conditions that have brought about this profound change is to be found in the transformation of the market structure. In advanced countries there has been a transformation into highly concentrated systems in which a few large firms dominate national and international markets. This has had a profound impact on the decision-making process. Under modern techniques of management, *research precedes decisions*. Careful surveys are being made of production and marketing potentials. The longer-run perspective is used because the very size of any additional investment requires a good amount of certainty that the long-range outlook justifies this commitment of resources. The aspects of risk and venture have been reduced to a minimum. They are in fact incompatible with the nature of technologically advanced large-scale enterprise. Hence participation in foreign development through the creation of wholly owned subsidiaries or the acquisition of already existing successful firms in foreign countries suggests itself as the safest method of investment under such circumstances.

Another change in decision making for economic growth is connected with the increasing role of the public sector in the promotion of growth and expansion, especially in emerging countries. Here social overhead capital must be created in order to make successful investments possible. There must be a build-up of road and transportation systems; the scope of education must be widened especially on the elementary level; water and energy resources must be developed. In many urban areas housing facilities for populations streaming in from the rural sector must be created. It follows that decision making under such circumstances requires the cooperation between government and business especially in those areas in which economic development is not carried out on a completely socialist model of growth. However, even in such cases there is often a de facto "coexistence" between public and private enterprises. In the 1960's the Soviet Union concluded a contract with the largest automobile manufacturing company in Italy, giving it a license to set up large-scale production facilities in Russia and to begin the mass production of low-priced cars to be sold in the Soviet Union. Socialist countries after World War II also in many instances contracted private firms in Europe for the delivery of complete production systems such as chemical plants.

This type of decision making always extends to the public sector. Furthermore, economic development generated according to this pattern does not depend upon private capital markets. It is financed out of retained earnings of private corporations, government loans and revenues collected in developing countries themselves. The latter source of investment funds has been particularly important in the Soviet type of economic development. A combination of high priorities for the build-up of heavy industry and the freezing of agricultural investment and income at a low level made it possible for the Soviet Union to finance industrialization by squeezing surpluses out even of a very depressed and neglected agricultural sector. In addition, for the first four decades, wages and consumer goods output were kept low so that even in industrial production internal resources accumulated that could be made available for further expansion.

We encounter here a second type of a bootstrap method of economic growth. The first type, we may recall, consisted of tax incentives and other concessions for private business investment. The other type, just described, is predicated on macroeconomic decision making, setting priorities with regard to development targets, speeding up certain sectors while slowing down others. The first type is merely setting the stage for economic development. It hopes for the forthcoming of many purely private investment decisions. The ensuing economic development would be spontaneous. Its direction would not be prearranged and its outcome not entirely predictable. The second bootstrap model of decision making requires the willingness and the political ability of a developing system to undergo measures of restraint and to submit voluntarily or otherwise to constraints on consumption levels. This has been called autonomous economic developments.

While this austerity pattern has been the characteristic of systems operating on principles of socialism in which all decisions are concentrated in the public sector, the setting up of priorities and restrictions is not inherent in socialism as such, but rather in the development requirements of a system trying to make a rapid transition to industrialization or modernization and expansion of a large but obsolescent system, Britain is an example. Now the imposition of such priorities on a system not operating under socialistic policies is made more difficult by the contradictions between this type of planning and timing of investment and the history and ideology of spontaneous economic development as it is being carried over from the perfectly competitive market system developing under conditions of political democracy. This is clearly shown in the difficulties encountered by the labor government in Britain to scale down excessive consumer spending in the 1960's.

Actually every situation of economic development is dealing with scarcities of social overhead capital, skilled labor, industrial equipment, and engineering and business know-how. It would be quite unrealistic to expect an automatic, nondirected response of resources to the injection of investment capital into a developing system without serious distortions between the various sectors and income groups. Very often initial increases of investment have led to a reinforcement rather than to a lessening of income disparities in developing countries. The additional money flow encouraged the purchase by established upper income classes of expensive automobiles and other costly consumer items. Unless there are restraints on imports of this type, the leakage from this kind of investment is bound to be very great. In this way the intent of economic aid, to assist developing countries in building up basic resources, in improving quality and diversity of agriculture output and initiating light domestic industries will be achieved only to a very limited extent.

Decision making for development in emerging countries cannot proceed from the assumption that these areas are approaching the so-called "take-off" phase which occurred in some European countries before the turn of the eighteenth century. In most of these areas the aftereffect of long prevailing land-labor accumulation systems and the weak development, if any, of prior internal capital accumulation render impossible the transfer of development models formulated in the historical context of Northwestern Europe and of the United States. In eighteenth century Europe, the middle class was fully developed. In many emerging countries today it is still in the initial stages of formation.

In view of these differences in the historical background of emerging countries, development decisions must be made more in a microeconomic frame of specific enterprises and projects than on the scale of reinforcing various sectors of the economy in huge macroeconomic aggregates. The latter method, especially if not accompanied by careful timing and restrictions, will only lead to the type of disequilibria already discussed. Specifically, this type of decision must focus on particular projects. It must pinpoint the particular enterprises, public or private, which must be built up with priority within the scope of a longer strategy of economic development. It should be noted that this pinpointing of economic aid and development has been more characteristic of economic aid extended by European countries to developing areas than of American programs. It also was employed by the Soviet Union in the 1950's when it was extending economic aid to Communist China by agreeing to set up about a hundred industrial production units in various manufacturing industries. Engineers from the Soviet Union came to China to supervise installation of machinery and initiate operation of this productive equpiment. These experts were recalled as Russian-Chinese tensions mounted. The largest example of a pinpointed type of economic development is the construction of the Aswan Dam in Egypt.

Generally speaking, decision making concentrating on specific projects rather than relying on multiplier effects of development funds given to established governments and their backers in emerging countries is the type of aid most suitable for those areas which must undergo sectoral-growth types of development as described at the beginning of this chapter. The other method can lead to premature factor transformation and the reinforcements of a dual structure of the economy, leaving great sectors of an emerging country in the subsistence part of the economy while modernizing the smaller market and industrial segment for the benefit of the few.

But economic development is bound to run into formidable problems even if no errors are made in the selection of strategies for economic development, if the impact of all the historical conditions outlined in the preceding chapter has been properly assessed, and if the appropriate model of economic growth, sectoral or factor transformation has been selected. We will turn our attentions to those factors in the next chapter.

chapter 4

Some Paradoxes of
Economic Development

Economic development in the late twentieth century occurs under multiple pressures of acceleration. The projected increase in the world population to about six billion by the year 2000 has created a permanent emergency condition in vast areas in which economic development has been retarded, such as in most parts of Latin America and in many areas of Africa and Asia. In highly advanced countries rapid technological change is bringing about accelerated factor transformation with its strong impact on the labor force, on educational requirements, and on the shape of the enterprise and of decision making. This speeding-up of processes of change on the real level of population, systems of production, and methods of business operations is pushed forward with great strength by the psychological factor of rising expectations. If economic development were strictly a problem of rational planning with purely technical aspects the only concern, adequate solutions would be available to relieve all these pressures before they become unmanageable. However, it is necessary to realize that strictly technical solutions of problems of economic development are inadequate. They are bound to solve one problem—such as low yields of traditional agricultural methods—only to create new problems, in this instance an agricultural surplus population. In advanced countries the inevitable further development of mechanization, automation in production, and public and business administration posits problems of pockets of unemployment, of state and local finance, and of rising cost and prices. Generally speaking, the optimistic assumption of nineteenth-century social and economic thought that reduction of scarcity and the general spread of rising living standards would relieve much of the social and individual pressures has already proved to be an illusion. The major issue that has to be faced squarely is whether economic policies for development merely shift severe problems from one sector of the system to another from purely economic to personal, educational, and group relations, or whether it is possible to devise problem-solving procedures which maintain social and economic balance as the economy is rising to higher levels of output.

In order to grasp the difficulties that are being encountered it is necessary to analyze in some detail certain clearly discernible paradoxes of economic development. At various stages of economic development unfavorable side effects can occur. They must be anticipated so that measures can be adopted to neutralize them. We will deal here with four of these dilemmas. Although they are not likely to occur simultaneously, they can appear in pairs or in other combinations of more than one. These paradoxes of economic development can focus on four major areas:

Population displacements
Runaway inflation
Ever-increasing labor-force participation
Widening gap between advanced and retarded countries

Before we deal with the paradoxes in some detail it is advisable to elaborate in a summary fashion on the four problem areas outlined above.

1. Increase in farm output is the indispensable prerequisite for maintaining and improving food-population ratios in most underdeveloped countries. Yet the very methods being used to bring about this development goal cause technological unemployment in agriculture and increase the pressure on nonagricultural employment opportunities and public and private urban facilities.
2. Economic development in emerging as well as in advancing countries requires increase in social overhead capital and in private and public investment in directly productive facilities. The overall demand for all kinds of services, educational, health and private increases. Greater outlays for nonproduction activities increase cost and tend to generate inflation. As development proceeds it becomes less and less cost-effective and required money outlays rise steeply.
3. As output potentials and actual levels of increase and the work week is being curtailed, aggregate demand for employment and for income is increasing. There is more leisure on one side and more need for income on the other side. Hence in countries undergoing great changes in productivity in the farm and nonfarm sector labor force participation far from decreasing is increasing.
4. The need for development is shared by advanced and emerging systems alike. Since the former have a tremendous head start, economic development has so far not reduced differentials between

industrialized and underdeveloped areas of the world. In fact the gap is widening thus creating the possibility of a continuation of vast international, interregional, and interracial inequalities. In a period of instant global communications and aroused awareness this paradox is potentially troublesome.

We will now discuss these four areas of paradoxical trends and structures separately.

AGRICULTURAL SURPLUSES AND RURAL SURPLUS POPULATIONS: A SURVEY OF PILOT REFORM PROJECTS

We have stressed in Chapter 3 that the acceleration of economic development in the last centuries went through three stages. During the first phase—the period we have come to call the first Industrial Revolution—while there were radical transformations in manufacturing and in transportation and communication, the rate of change in agricultural techniques and in land distribution was extremely small. Smaller-scale units in farming often engaged in more intensive land utilization such as truck and dairy farming. Larger agricultural holdings especially in Central, Eastern, and Southern Europe as well as in Latin America were oriented toward more extensive methods of land use. When Werner Sombart wrote his study on the German economy in the nineteenth and at the beginning of the twentieth century* he stated in his chapter on agriculture that even in large-scale agricultural enterprises capitalistic methods have made only slow progress. He also stressed that in the last hundred years there had virtually been no change in the structure of German agriculture.

One aspect of this lag in agricultural development, especially in Europe, was the trend of agricultural cost to rise, as the population increased and as the rapidly growing urban and industrial sector of the economy brought about a strong demand for agricultural products. This was the cause of the various methods in support of domestic agriculture inaugurated by European governments in the latter part of the nineteenth century. High protective tariffs were erected in order to isolate domestic farm prices from world market pressures and to enable farmers to continue high cost operations without fear of foreign competition. It is easy to see why these tariff walls enabled agriculture to continue to operate without

*Werner Sombart, *Die Deutsche Dolkswirtschaft im 19 Hahrhundert und im Anfang des 20.* Stuttgart, 1954.

being forced into technological innovations. Only after World War II with the formation of the European Common Market was there some change in this type of agricultural protectionism. Tariffs have been moved to the frontiers of this new larger and supranational system while they have been eliminated internally. However, former colonial and plantation economies continue to suffer from large fluctuations of prices of crops and raw materials in the world market.

Despite the very slow progress in agricultural techniques during the nineteenth century, employment opportunities in rural areas were not sufficient to take care of the rapidly growing population in need of income. For this reason there was a continuous flow, especially of younger people from the agricultural to the rapidly rising industrial sector of the system. Large-scale agricultural unemployment and rural underemployment was prevented by two factors—first, steady demand for additional workers in industry, and second, relatively high demands for farm workers due to the slowness of progress in agriculture.

This rapidly increasing demand for workers in industry can be easily demonstrated by a study of the growth on the nonagricultural labor force in Germany within a twenty-five year period between 1882 and 1907. Employment in mining doubled. The number of workers in the metal industries and shipbuilding showed an even higher rate of increase. The electrical products industry had barely started in 1882. Between 1895 and 1907 employment in this branch of manufacturing increased by 500 percent. In the same twelve-year period employment in the building trades also doubled.* Similar developments occurred in the United States. In the year 1900 nonagricultural employment was 15.9 million; in 1907 it had risen to 21.7 million. In the same period agricultural employment in the United States was still rising, but in this period it increased only by 500,000.†

These figures show the validity of the two points made above. If factor transformation assumes momentum in the industrial sector while it is very slow in the agricultural sector, increased labor supply brought forth by rising population can be accommodated with comparative ease in the expanding labor force. This is particularly evident when activities such as mining and road building are growing rapidly, in which it is possible to employ unskilled labor and give them on-the-job training. The slight increase in agricultural employment in the United States at the beginning of

---

*Sombart, *op. cit.*, Appendix 22.
†*Long-Term Economic Growth, 1860-1965*, U.S. Department of Commerce, Series A, 83-A 93.

this century which is in such sharp contrast to the tremendous decline in employment in that sector after World War II demonstrates that in that period increases in agricultural output were due more to sectoral growth patterns than to factor transformation. The agricultural revolution had not as yet set in and it was necessary to increase the factor labor together with agricultural machinery in order to achieve higher output levels.

The American experience of the first decade of this century shows a time sequence in economic development which enables a growing labor force to adjust without grave inbalances to industrialization. The time lead in factor transformation in industry and the time lag in agriculture created sufficient leeway to go through this phase of economic development without causing serious problems of rural underemployment or unemployment. Once this sequence pattern is changed—as it was in the United States in the 1950's and 1960's and is being translated into a chain of transformations in which the continued agricultural revolution and the second Industrial Revolution begin to operate simultaneously—an advanced system is suddenly confronted with stubborn problems of pockets of unemployment persisting even while on a macroscale the labor market seems to be in balance.

Factor transformation in the industrial sector in advanced Western countries was at least until World War II based primarily on investment decisions made in the private sector. In the Soviet Union and later in socialist countries adopting the Soviet type of economic development factor transformation, the accumulation of capital through the building up of socialized industries was accomplished through the device of centralized planning, usually in the form of five-year plans. This type of controlled development can be called forced industrialization because it amounted to an attempt to compress in a comparatively short period of time processes of economic growth which had been stretched out much longer in Western countries. While the process of decision making in capitalist and in socialist countries was entirely different, nevertheless actual patterns of development had in common the lead-lag pattern in factor transformation with the industrial sector going ahead and agriculture for many decades staying behind. In the Soviet Union and some other Soviet-type countries such as East Germany, agriculture was not only permitted to lag behind but was actually going downward due to enforced collectivization of farms and the ensuing initial declines in output. Eventually output levels increased. But whereas total farm employment in the United States in 1958 was only 7.5 million of whom only 2 million were hired workers and the rest family workers, the Soviet Union still needed 25 million workers in agriculture,

18 million on collective farms, and 7 million on state farms. In both countries farm employment has declined sharply since then. In the United States it was down to 5.2 million in 1966. The main point, however, in this comparison is that a time lead of industrialization avoids the accumulation of an agricultural surplus population.

It is easy to understand why countries entering into processes of economic development in the late twentieth century would like to emulate this sequence in economic development. However, it is necessary to stress the great differences in historical conditions between Western countries and the Soviet Union on the one side and currently emerging areas in the rest of the world. A study of these differences will show that an imitation of these patterns of development is not feasible and that it becomes necessary to face squarely the rapidly developing paradoxical situation in Latin America and many parts of Africa.

While in the currently advanced countries of the West and East there was a great deal of poverty in rural sectors, conditions of the farm population in the eighteenth and nineteenth centuries were far better in terms of nutrition and housing than they are today in vast sections of emerging countries. Despite the dire forecasts of Thomas Malthus there was no actual imbalance between population growth and food supply, except for isolated cases such as the Great Hunger in Ireland.* Furthermore, as shipping facilities increased during that period European countries were able to import ever-increasing quantities of farm products from abroad, because they placed great stress on the building up of export industries and of foreign investment with which to earn foreign exchange for the import of food and raw materials from overseas. By processing these materials into industrial exports, Europe was operating under favorable terms of trade throughout its own period of industrialization.

The basic situation in countries starting economic development in the late twentieth century is entirely different. As a carryover of former colonial and plantation economies, many countries in Latin America and also in Africa were operating the economy on the basis of one or two major crops to be sold on the world market. In Brazil the export of coffee accounted for 44 percent of the total exports. Even higher ratios prevailed in Cuba with its traditional monoculture of sugar. As a result of such a one-sided system of large-scale agriculture there was in these countries very little diversification in farming. Dietary standards were low for the large rural masses due to the lack of variety in food.

*Cecil Woodham-Smith, *The Great Hunger: Ireland 1845-1849,* New York, Harper & Row, 1963.

Development designs to bring about greater diversity in agriculture and in nutrition in these areas which are also characterized by a rapid natural growth of the population are encountering a dilemma. If methods were adopted such as were applied with spectacular success in the United States in the twentieth century or even if policies were carried out somewhat along the more recent Soviet type of initiating greater efficiency and productivity of agriculture, the current difficulties in agriculture in these countries would be solved only at the expense of creating even more puzzling social and economic problems elsewhere.

In the United States, and after World War II in many European countries, the number of farm units has dropped sharply while at the same time the average size of the farms has increased. Small farms are no longer viable economically because they cannot support the cost of modern farm equipment. In order to make the utilization of advanced farm technology and production methods feasible, the farming units must be brought to an optimum relationship between yields and unit cost of farm production. We have already seen that this has led to a radical factor transformation and drastic declines in farm employment. Although Soviet agriculture was long managed according to altogether different and often erroneous principles, farm developments in the Soviet Union and in the United States have nevertheless in common the accelerating trend toward the elimination of smaller units in farming and their merging into much larger systems. During 1950-51 the number of collective farms in the Soviet Union was reduced from 250,000 to 123,000. Over the years further reductions were carried out. More recently only 36,000 collective farms remained. At the same time the giant state farms, numbering 12,000, were continuously being increased and the total land area under cultivation was still being augmented.

Agricultural development policies have to cope with an economic paradox generated by the agricultural revolution itself: the very means of overcoming basic deficiencies in quantity and quality of output require higher productivity per farm worker and, therefore, a reduction of the agricultural labor force itself. This has been the case in all countries making rapid advances in agriculture, even in the Soviet Union. Now in countries which are at the same time still completing their first industrial revolution or have already entered their second industrial revolution, the radical restructuring of the labor force required by the very nature of factor transformation in farming merely shifts employment from the agricultural to the nonagricultural sector of the economy.

Newly developing countries will find it impossible to initiate rates of industrialization of the U.S. or USSR type within a period of time short enough to absorb masses of rural people that would be displaced by radical factor transformation in the agricultural sector. In these cases the conversion of food deficits into agricultural surpluses would be achieved only by the transfer of poverty on the land into destitution in ghettos and shanty-towns of urban areas.

The avoidance of this grave threat to social and economic stability must be one of the primary goals of development policies in these areas. In some *Latin American* countries, pilot reforms have been initiated to establish higher-output goals and a better product mix in farming without cutting drastically overall employment in agriculture.

The land reform which was inaugurated in *Chile* in 1967 under President Frei can serve as an example. Under this bill the government appropriated from the big landowners about 15 million acres of land which was considered underutilized. This did not mean total expropriation of the Communist type but enforced redistribution of land up to now used only for extensive farming. The reform of 1967 provides for compensation of landowners with an immediate payment of 10 percent of the current value. The rest is to be paid in thirty-year bonds.

The ultimate goal of the reform is to create individually owned farms of an average size of twenty-five acres. In direct contrast to Soviet agricultural policies, which first distributed land to peasants at the start of the revolution and then forced the farmers into collectivization, in Chile the reverse procedure has been adopted. Agricultural workers living on expropriated land are to form initially a collective in order to plan properly for crops, soil improvement, and agricultural equipment. But once a beginning has been made in crop diversification and improvement in agricultural productivity the individual farms are slated as the new permanent form of agriculture in that part of Chile.

It is hoped that in this way a very large number of landless farm workers will be permanently settled in farms of their own in which they will contribute to a substantial overall increase in agricultural output. While the target figure of one million seems to be very large, it should be pointed out that even if this goal is only approximated, the relative farm population of Chile would far exceed that of the United States where factor transformation in agriculture is the most radical. The Chilean plan provides for the setting up of elected committees of farmers to make joint decisions with regard to crops and agricultural techniques. It is interesting to note that this plan has provided even for the inclusion of the former land proprietor in these committees. In this way an organizational structure is being created which should enable a transition from extensive, latifundia style systems of farming to the more intensive and diversified methods envisaged by land reform without the discontinuities and sharp declines in output encountered in the Soviet Union in the 1930's.

Large-scale expropriation of sugar plantations and the expulsion of owners and expert managers during the Castro revolution in *Cuba* brought about severe dislocations and disruptions in the sugar economy. For a number of years, output continued far below prerevolutionary levels and the proclaimed agricultural objectives of the revolution, especially crop diversification and the development of a livestock and dairy industry was retarded. In fact, the monoculture of sugar became even more vital especially after the Soviet Union pledged itself to purchase the crop at prices above the world market level. Despite these setbacks, progress was made after 1965 toward diversification through the building up of herds of cattle and the encouragement of fruit and vegetable growing. All these efforts required a great deal of labor and during peak harvesting seasons in the 1960's segments of the nonagricultural population, especially students, had to be "mobilized" to help out with bringing in the crops. As elsewhere in developing countries of Latin America, these moves toward a restructuring of the agricultural sector were accompanied in Cuba with an extension of rural school systems. The general trend of the plan indicates that higher levels of output are attempted without creating at least for the time being an agricultural surplus population.

Another example of dealing with agricultural development and a general economic growth of a neglected area through reform rather than through revolution is to be found in recent developments in the Northeastern part of *Brazil*. This area consists of nine states in the easternmost section of Brazil completely located in the tropical zone. About one-third of the total population of Brazil, 27 million people, lived there in the 1960's. Their per capita income was only half of what it is in the more prosperous southern part of the country. In 1966 it was only $180 per annum. Historically the area had been used for extensive types of agriculture such as sugar plantations and huge cattle ranches. After the abolishment of slavery in 1889 coffee was grown as well as cocoa and cotton. The world market prices for these crops are subject to very wide fluctuations. Especially in the period between the two World Wars this created great instability in the economic situation and particularly in employment. At the same time the population continued its very rapid growth. Economic conditions, especially in the hinterland of this area, continued in a state of permanent depression. As a result the large masses of this rural population facing underemployment or complete lack of job opportunities began to migrate to urban centers such as Recife, the original capital of Brazil in colonial times. They also drifted to the more prosperous Southern part of the country where they added to the population of the shanties or favelas on the hills surrounding Rio de Janiero.

In 1960 a Brazilian federal agency was set up to implement plans for the upgrading of this underdeveloped area. This government body, called Sudene, acted as a coordinating agency trying to align public expenditures, private investment, technical assistance and foreign aid in the working out of priorities and time sequences in the overall development design. Actually the situation in that part of Brazil was so desperate that emergency relief measures had to be initiated at the beginning of the program. Food supplies were distributed to poverty-stricken areas by United States foreign aid and United Nations agencies; loans were given for these immediate relief purposes by the Inter-American Development Bank. Obviously relief is not the answer to long-range economic development objectives.

As the development plans in the Brazilian Northeast assume shape it becomes apparent that industrialization is to play an important role in absorbing locally the surplus population. Here we again encounter aspects of the bootstrap model discussed in the previous chapter. Brazilian companies are promised a 50 percent reduction in their corporation tax liability if they invest an equivalent amount in enterprises in the Northeast. However, these investments must be channeled through the Development Agency, in order to avoid distortions in the growth pattern. Around Recife about forty industrial enterprises have been established primarily in light industries such as paint, ceramics, and consumer goods. In 1967 industrial plants representing a total investment of $75 million were under construction in the area of Salvador. Among these enterprises were processing plants for woods, fibers, and metals. A small steel plant with an annual capacity of 138,000 tons was being planned. Fuel was to be supplied in part by natural gas to be developed nearby. Very important for development projects of this type is the improvement of water supply and the generation of electric power. Already in 1954 a hydroelectric plant was established on the São Francisco River and the plans provided for an increase of its capacity to 975,000 kilowatts by 1970.

In the *Philippines* the Spanish conquest also led to the setting up of large-scale feudalistic haciendas especially in the most fertile parts of Luzon Island. The termination of Spanish rule in 1898 did not change this basic structure. The mass of the rural population consisted of sharecroppers having often to pay up to 50 percent of their crops to the land owner. In the 1960's reforms were initiated, small in scale, but significant for future patterns. Payments to landlords were limited to 25 percent of the average crops of the preceding years. This was also the maximum of future payments regardless of expected improvements in yields due to better seeds and farming methods. In this way the income of the farmers is bound to increase in the long run whereas the revenues of the landlord will remain more or less fixed. Gradually this will bring about a better distribution of income than prevailed in the past due to the survival into the twentieth century of feudalistic forms of land ownership and management.

Iran is another country in which distribution of land has been carried out to a large extent in order to liquidate feudalism. In this case the reform movement was from the top down, at the initiative of the Shah who realized that structural changes were urgently required if his country was to preserve its independence from the Soviet Union to the North and the unstable Arab nations to the southwest. The Shah incurred determined opposition from the landed aristocracy which had managed to survive as a ruling feudal group even in the middle of the twentieth century. In order to set the stage for more general reforms, the Shah agreed in 1951 that the peasants in 2,000 villages located on his own estate be given land and transformed into independent farmers. Eventually legislation was enacted freeing 15 million people from feudalistic agricultural arrangements and giving them land of their own. Simultaneously agricultural cooperatives were set up to enable farmers to improve their resources and to afford mechanized equipment.

The preceding description* of recent reform and development measures in Chile and Brazil, the Philippines and Iran, shows that a proper mixing of intensification of agriculture and industrialization is the method indicated to counteract the inherent dilemma of large developing countries which must increase food output on the one hand and must supply employment opportunities for a rapidly growing population on the other. In terms of the basic models of sectoral growth and of factor transformation, this means that a proper proportion must be worked out for the simultaneous activation of development of these two types of expansion. Radical factor transformation as it has occurred first in American agriculture and as now promoted in the common-market countries is not a suitable technique in

*The information about agricultural developments in Brazil, Chile, and the Philippines was taken from extensive reports which appeared in the *New York Times,* January 30, 1967 (Brazil), July 17, 1967 (Chile), and April 12, 1968 (Philippines). In a rapidly moving situation it seems permissible to refer to such sources rather than wait for scholarly publications.

most developing countries. Rather, it becomes necessary to devise methods which increase agricultural productivity drastically without rendering small and medium-sized agricultural units economically obsolete. The concept of feasibility in economic development must be extended to the social impact of technological production possibilities in farming. The social cost of large-scale displacement of rural populations and the consequent overburdening of the resources of urban areas must be considered in any calculus of investment and land-distribution patterns in agriculture. Furthermore industrialization must proceed primarily for the purpose of enriching and enlarging local markets. Industrialization merely for the purpose of generating employment opportunities—or, as it has happened occasionally, to enhance the prestige of government—is ultimately self-defeating. Here we encounter another very important aspect in this basically paradoxical situation: the problem of timing. Population pressures indicate that time is running out and that resources, output, and employment opportunities must be increased now in order to keep the overall situation manageable. But these policies require longer periods of time until they show the first results in a tangible form. The tension created by accumulating population pressures and the slow response to them in terms of economic improvements can be channeled into nonviolent action only if it is possible to communicate to rural masses effectively that basic changes are underway and will result in substantial improvements at a somewhat distant but clearly defined point in the future. Hardships can be accepted if it is clearly understood that they are transitory and that the future is open to improvement.

DEVELOPMENT, INVESTMENT, AND INFLATION

In many countries attempting economic development a condition of galloping inflation has prevailed over long periods of time. The extent of this rapid rise in prices in some Latin American countries is shown in the table below. It should be noted that in some other Latin American countries price developments have been far less pronounced. On the basis of 1958 = 100, prices in Venezuela had risen only by 7 percent in 1964; the increase in Mexico was 14 percent. Inasmuch as these countries continued on a growth path during that period, it is evident that economic development does not necessarily lead to extreme rates of inflation.

Galloping inflation brings about serious distortions in the distribution of real income which in the long run are bound to limit the growth

Consumer Price Index in
Selected Latin American Countries
(1958 = 100)

Year	Argentina	Brazil	Chile	Columbia
1948	14	25	5	45
1955	54	60	40	71
1956	61	73	63	76
1957	76	87	83	87
1959	214	137	139	107
1960	272	185	155	111
1961	309	256	167	121
1962	396	390	190	124
1963	491	675	274	164
1964	600	1,266	400	192

Source: Statistical Yearbook of the United Nations, 1965

potential of a developing economy. In such a setting the property owners and those who have tangible assets such as inventories can protect themselves against the depreciation of the currency. Wage and salary earners are bound to lag behind almost continously in their purchasing power. It seems essential, therefore, to prevent this type of inflation which ultimately is bound to negate the effects of whatever economic progress has been achieved.

We have seen already that it is possible to go ahead with economic development without ultimately crossing the threshold of accelerating inflation with all its adverse consequences. In advanced countries policies have been adopted occasionally to deliberately slow down economic development in order to avoid inflationary pressures. This was done for instance in France in the early 1960's. From the viewpoint of highly industrialized countries in which there are no internal population pressures, the paradox of growth and inflation has sometimes been viewed under the aspects of a shifting of policy priorities from full employment to price stability. It is being said in this context that in order to prevent inflation it might be necessary to pay the price of some unemployment. It should be obvious that such alternatives do not exist in developing countries which are already suffering from high degrees of unemployment.

In order to analyze the problems of development and of monetary stability which arise under such circumstances, it is necessary to clarify the underlying concepts of inflation. In fact, no type of monetary policy can succeed which is not firmly grounded on an adequate theoretical frame of reference. We are not being helped in analyzing the problem by oversimplified generalizations about the phenomenon of inflation. If, as is often done, any measurable increase in prices is classified as "inflation," we have barred an access to analyzing specific problems requiring solutions on various levels of economic development. Neither is the distinction between "cost-push" or "demand-pull" types of inflation particularly helpful. In advanced countries it is possible to raise wages and additional costs of legal or contractual fringe benefits without raising unit labor costs whenever there are corresponding gains in productivity. In those countries demand pull in a peacetime economy is actually the prerequisite to keep a technologically progressive system on an equilibrium growth path. In a cold or limited war setting of such a highly developed system, aggregate spending emanating from the public sector is bound to inaugurate great pressures on prices. A further analysis of this situation will give us an insight into basic structures which, with some modifications, also operate in most developing countries.

Increases in aggregate spending for national defense and limited wars generate high levels of employment. Wages and salaries rise steeply because this type of spending translates itself into demand for highly skilled and highly paid manpower. In this way additional purchasing power is generated which exercises pressures on the prices for consumer goods and services and on the products purchased by government. Generally speaking, any expansion of aggregate purchasing power which is not translated into corresponding increases of output of consumer goods in the private sector and into residential construction is apt to generate income derived from the employment connected with nonprivate production goods and services. This in turn is bound to generate excess purchasing power and to lead to an "overheating" of the economy.

In developing countries it is unlikely that the distortion in the generating of total income is caused by cold- or limited-war spending. However, income generated by investment essential to economic development such as hydroelectric projects, road building, or public and industrial construction have the same income-generating effect as heavy defense spending in advanced countries. The wage sector in the economy expands rapidly and as a result the total money stream increases faster than the domestic output of consumer goods and services. It follows that all situations of economic development in countries in which the consumer sector has been weak prior to the start of policies designed to inaugurate economic growth have a *built-in inflation potential*. This is the prevailing condition in economic development everywhere in the late twentieth century. In this way the situation differs greatly from the period of the first industrial revolution in Western countries which could look back on hundreds of years of a slow growth of consumer-goods production prior to the acceleration of economic development.

Here we encounter another paradox of economic development which must be clearly understood in order to be handled properly. On the one hand economic development has an inflationary potential. On the other, inflation is bound to freeze or even accentuate income disparities. The way out of this dilemma must start with the acknowledgment that economic development under conditions typical of emerging countries today cannot be reconciled with rigid price stability. To pursue growth targets while at the same time attempting to keep prices unchanged is illusory. The realistic approach to the situation is to recognize the inflation potential and then devise policies to manage it. *Galloping inflation*—that is, a completely unchecked and ever-accelerating rise in prices brought about by a continuous increase in money supply and credit—is hardly a method of managing the inflation potential. It is a surrender to the inherent monetary pressures in economic development. There are a number of examples in recent history (for instance in Germany in 1923 and in 1948) in which inflationary situations were terminated overnight by retirement of the inflated currency and a replacement with new money at a drastically lower denomination. In Germany this was accompanied in 1948 by the conversion of savings and checking accounts to the new monetary units. But such a drastic cure operates to the disadvantage of savers and of wage and salary workers while at the same time it favors debtors—including the government which has generated a large public debt during the inflationary period, and businesses that hold large inventories produced with the outlay of bad money but which can now be sold for good money. There are two alternatives to this undesirable type of extreme inflation: *repressed inflation* and carefully *controlled inflation.*

Repressed inflation does not eliminate the inflationary pull of economic development but drives it, as it were, underground. The most outstanding example of repressed inflation over a long period of time has been given by the Soviet Union. Another case was the economic techniques used by the Nazis in the years of their hectic armament drive preceding World War II. Generally speaking, monetary policies in wartime fall under this method of managing inflation.

One of the cornerstones of repressed inflation is a comprehensive wage and salary freeze. This does not mean a complete halt to the growth of aggregate wages and salaries which can grow somewhat as a result of upgrading of jobs and of overtime. However, this will allow only for small changes. Another cornerstone would be a freezing of the output of consumer goods and services. In this way prices in the consumer sector can be held in line without actually introducing price control. It should be noted further that in the case of Germany as well as in the Soviet Union repressed inflation occurred while rents were frozen. It was possible under those circumstances to keep increases in the consumer index comparatively stable. The "underground" aspect of repressed inflation in Germany led to the creation of an ever-increasing public debt which, however, through ingenious but ultimately disastrous manipulations was dressed up as a private commercial debt of dummy government corporations placing most of the orders for defense materials and paying for them with promissory notes purchased by the Central Bank. In this way what was in reality huge government deficit spending appeared in the accounts as an extension of commercial credit to allegedly private corporations.

Under rigid systems of repressed inflation black markets are bound to develop in which goods are being bought and sold at generally inflated prices. In Communist countries such black markets have often been tolerated. After World War II in the course of a currency reform, Soviet black market millionaires lost virtually all of their earnings. But while it lasted, the black market was the underground aspect of repressed inflation in the Soviet Union.

In the United States inflation was repressed during World War II through the system of wage and price controls. Wages were not frozen but could be increased only with the consent of the War Labor Board. At the same time the other aspect of repressed inflation, a curtailment of the output of consumer goods and services could be carried out easily. There was no production of new automobiles for private use. There was a standstill in residential construction. Even with these restrictions, aggregate wages moved up through an increase in total employment, through upgrading and overtime. As a result, the rate of savings increased very steeply so that at the end of World War II consumers had built up large potential purchasing power. The availability of these funds to satisfy delayed consumer demands following the end of the war explains why the widely expected "primary postwar depression" never occurred in the United States.

As a result of the stabilization policy, inflationary pressures were held under check in the United States. On the basis of the period 1957-59 = 100 the consumer price index in 1941 was 51.3 and in 1945 it was 62.7. In the period immediately following cessation of hostilities prices rose much faster. In 1949 they had already reached 83. The outbreak of the Korean war in 1950 caused a rise of the consumer price index from 83.8 percent in 1950 to 91.5 percent in 1951. In the latter period the pressures caused by increased military spending were not accompanied by adequate stabilization measures. Hence at that time there was danger of a drift into galloping inflation.

Controlled inflation differs from repressed inflation by frankly admitting that prices are bound to rise. No attempts are being made to control prices by tying them to a particular level and to prevent any and all increases in wages. The general policy tends to keep purchasing power in line with rising prices and to prevent a distortion in the relations between the various income shares. Controlled inflation is frequently associated with plans to increase industrial capacity substantially in a comparatively short period of time. This was the case in France in the 1950's when the four-year plans for economic expansion of basic industries, such as steel, chemicals, and electronics got under way. In that period residential construction, though badly needed, was still limited. The adjustment of wages through rising prices was done through an increase in official minimum wages. Since wages of all other workers were defined in percentages above the minimum wage, any change in the minimum wage automatically also put into effect a rise in all other wages.

Actually, the yardstick that must be employed in order to measure the impact of inflation is the behavior of per capita income in a constant money unit. Whenever there is accelerated inflation of the galloping type wages and other forms of money income will not keep up with the continuous erosion of the purchasing power of money. There will be an actual decline in per capita personal income. However, when policies of repressed or controlled inflation work out as intended, the net result in terms of real per capita income will be real increase per annum reflecting the general growth of the economy.

In the United States monetary policies have been employed at various times in the period after World War II to curb inflation through increasing interest rates and reserve requirements. It was hoped that in this way prices could be kept reasonably stable. Attempts to hold wages down to 3.2 percent increases annually as was suggested by the Council of Economic Advisors until late in 1966 failed not because the concept of issuing guidelines for collective bargaining was wrong but as a result of an erroneous analysis of the impact of the transformation of the labor force, especially its continuous upgrading on the relation between productivity and wages.

Despite the continuous rise in prices in the United States and the public agonizing about inflation, the fact remains that disposable personal income in constant 1958 prices rose from $1,646 in 1950 to $2,391 in

1967. That means that while the population was rising in that same period by roughly 47 million from 152,271,000 in 1950 to 199,118,000 in 1967 the per capita income in constant dollars still went up by more than $700 during that period. The experience of most advanced industrial countries including the Soviet Union is along the same lines although increases were less spectacular.

On a more general level this post-World War II development proves conclusively that while rising prices cannot be avoided in a period of rapid economic development, it is entirely possible in industrial countries to keep the growth in per capita personal income abreast of these price trends. We arrive at the conclusion that in developing situations in areas where there is already a differentiated structure in the production and in the consumer sector there is no irreconcilable conflict between price developments and real economic growth on a level of an equitable distribution of the incidence of rising prices.

In developing countries there are greater difficulties in maintaining a favorable ratio between price increases and improvements in real per capita income. Unlike advanced countries, the economic structure in emerging countries is not based on a broad consumer goods production sector. Hence the comparatively rapid increase of the money flow cannot easily be dammed in by a rapid rise in the domestic output of consumer goods and services. In countries trying to go through successive stages of economic development according to a free-market model, funds accumulating in the country, especially through the influx of loans from abroad and economic aid, will leak to a considerable extent into the purchase of imported high-priced consumer items such as automobiles, motorcycles, television sets, and expensive household durables. In such an uncontrolled situation the real income of the vast masses of the population will continue to lag behind while the revenues of a small part of the population employed in trade, in developing industries or engaged in politics will go up steeply. This unstable situation is often enhanced in those developing countries which have historically been engaged in one- or two-crop agricultural economies and whose exports even today are subject to downward pressures on agricultural prices in world markets.

Under such conditions a control of inflation becomes an urgent necessity. It requires in the first place efficient fiscal management and a tax system that siphons off the excess gains which accrue to those who can derive direct benefits from their participation as executives and businessmen in the modern sector of a developing economy. Monetary policies must strike a balance between the need of facilitating investments through low interest rates and the inherent danger of the generation of excess purchasing power through the failure of connecting monetary expansion with specific growth and development targets. Control of inflation in such a setting also requires a restriction of high-priced consumer goods imports and a concentration on the purchase of machinery and other items conducive to increasing the productivity of the economy. In recent years some countries have made significant progress in improving the import-export ratio. In 1965 and 1966 exports of Argentina and of Brazil exceeded imports, whereas in an earlier period the reverse had been true. Another aspect of controlling inflation is the deliberate building up of domestic industries which eventually will be able to substitute domestic products for foreign ones. In Brazil the import substitution of automobiles produced within the country has been particularly successful.

Controlled inflation aiming at across-the-board spread of improvements in real income presupposes an effective and honest public administration capable of administering fiscal, monetary, and trade policies without leakages due to inefficient enforcement and corruption. It follows that one of the most urgent priorities in developing countries is the setting up of such administrative systems. Inflation cannot be controlled if precapitalistic business ethics permitting gratuities to officials, kickbacks, nepotism, and similar practices continue to go unchallenged. Such behavior was virtually taken for granted in feudalistic economic and social structures in many parts of the world. It was connected with a collective egotism of large, cohesive families and the widespread idea that those holding political and economic power are entitled to use it for their own advantage and exercise influence in favor of their supporters and families. Development designs for countries having to control inflation as part of their successful move toward higher levels of output and income must take into account the historical background of prevailing administrative and business ethics. It must be realized in this connection that the rise of a professional, disinterested civil service, not connected with the private economic structure and economically secured by tenure and lifelong, legally guaranteed pension income, is a product only of the modern state as it emerged in Europe in the sixteenth and seventeenth centuries. Civil-service systems operating with the professional ethics of noninvolvement in economics and complete rejection of material rewards other than those provided by law cannot be created overnight, and it cannot be assumed that emerging nations which were outside this special tradition will automatically adopt these standards in the civil services they are building up. It follows that a successful control of inflation is not merely an economic problem.

It is subject to solution only if the administrative preconditions and requirements are understood clearly. Obviously even a public administration operating with this type of ethics will experience deviations from these standards and scandals. However, under such conditions inefficiency and graft will no longer be taken for granted. Whenever they occur they will be uprooted.

In view of the complexity of administering controlled inflation in developing countries, direct production assistance in foreign-aid programs is far preferable to general allocations to foreign governments. Such assistance programs have a far lower leakage factor than other more general forms of economic aid, such as import subsidies.

We have seen in this section that economic development is bound to generate an upward pull in prices no matter whether it is a case of a further advance of an already industrialized system or whether we are dealing with the situation in an emerging country. It should be noted that this trend of prices indicates the limitations of the effect of savings on factor cost and on prices. Theoretically the expectation seems to be justified that factor transformation, especially the greater use of capital and the declining labor requirements would have the effect of keeping prices relatively stable while levels of output rise steeply.

But in order for this to come true, the market would have to operate close to conditions of perfect competition. However, the very nature of factor transformation, the ever-increasing capital requirements are a powerful agent in the trend toward business concentration and the transition from perfect to imperfect competition. This change of the structure of the market as countries achieve ever higher levels of industrialization is one factor in the failure of the price system to maintain previous lower levels. Another factor is the transformation in advanced countries of the old blue-collar, manual, production-worker economy into a new white-collar, clerical, administrative economy. As economic development proceeds to ever higher levels, the nonproduction labor force component rises sharply. There is a proliferation of activities only indirectly or at least not immediately connected with current output of goods and services which, however, must be financed out of the sales to ultimate consumers. Weapons systems, new types of automobiles, airplanes and the like slated to become operative within ten or fifteen years are now being researched, designed, and tested by highly paid experts. Counseling activities, public relations campaigns, and the expansion of educational systems require nonproduction employment on an ever-broadening scale. While the use of modern equipment such as photostatic reproductions of printed matter and computers have led to a considerable speeding up of the production of documents and correspondence, the share of all these administrative and bureaucratic systems in total factor costs is rising steadily. In this connection we must also take into account the rising cost of equipment related to the need of installing increasingly "efficient" office machinery.

This new mix in the composition of the factor labor does indeed bring about a cost-push situation. In the 1960's the increasing cost of nonproduction labor has offset the trend of production labor cost to remain stable as a result of rapidly rising output per man-hour.

The conditions which are conducive to a rise in prices in emerging and in developing countries are entirely different. But both basic patterns of economic development have in common this trend toward a secular rise in price levels and this despite the fact that in these two cases productivity is continuing to rise. Under such circumstances the main goal of monetary policies and wage guidelines must focus on the protection of real income. The latter must be kept moving upward because otherwise economic development will soon end up in stagnation. This emphasis on the significance of a proper rate of growth of real income makes it absolutely necessary to prevent the rise in prices to accelerate to the point where inflation would reach the "galloping" phase. On the other hand, the stress on real income should guard the policy makers against undue restraints on development, especially in the investment sector merely because prices are rising.

Controlled inflation is therefore the only feasible policy in all developmental situations. In emerging countries this may entail restriction on the consumer sector while emphasizing the investment sector. In advanced countries restraints on consumption would have to be used with great care. Only if consumer credit being currently extended threatened to exceed repayments in an ever-increasing proportion would there be an occasion to correct this imbalance. Increases in interest rates as a monetary device to curb the heating up of a boom situation has proved to be a double-edged sword in highly advanced countries. The need to meet increasing interest payments may in itself develop into an additional factor in the cost-push situation. The intent of a steep rise in interest rates—namely, a restraint on further price rises—may actually have opposite effects.

To sum up, monetary policies must be brought into context with the structure of economic development. Price movements cannot be viewed in isolation. They must be seen in their impact on real income shares, their relation to each other, and to the trends in real output and improvements in the overall social and economic structure.

OPEN-ENDEDNESS OF ECONOMIC DEVELOPMENT

We have seen in Chapter 1 that nineteenth-century thought on economic development was visualizing a final very prosperous stage of an economic system settling down into an presumably blissful state of economic stagnation. There was unbounded belief in the beneficial effects of social and economic progress always with a mixture of the expectations of an ideal end phase. Now one of the greatest paradoxes of economic development as it emerges in the latter part of the twentieth century consists of the fact that even the most advanced system cannot afford to stand still. It is therefore necessary to analyze in some detail the relations between various patterns of economic development, the structure of employment and the aggregate demand for income.

In simple, undifferentiated economics in which most families are not only "spending units" but also production units in the fields and in ancestral villages and homes, economic activities are embedded in a total life situation. Activities may stretch from dusk to dawn but the pace is slow and according to the seasons there will be wide variations in the actual work being carried out. Looking at this situation through the conceptual lenses of comtemporary labor-market statistics, the normal state of underdeveloped countries may be considered as underemployment. It should be noted, however, that the very concept of underemployment carries with it a number of assumptions that are not necessarily part of the culture system of a primitive economic society. Among these assumptions are the desire of people to achieve maximum returns from factors of production, the existence of something like a normal work week or working hours per year, and the demand for continuous improvement in living conditions.

In fact, economic development even of a slow rate of growth cannot get underway unless at least one of these assumptions becomes a motivating force in actual economic behavior. As economic growth is starting and people will experience some initial improvement in their life situation, employment patterns will begin to change. Work will become better organized and more intensive. Alternate production plans will be set up for the off seasons. On the one hand economic development requires a greater input of labor in order to get started. On the other hand, as development rises to higher levels the demand for employment opportunities will rise rather steeply. The problem then shifts to an emerging labor market and to the maintenance of a balance between employment opportunities and the demand for work. We have seen that this equilibrium can be maintained easily whenever technological labor displacement in the farm sector can be compensated for by the rapid growth of the market and industrial economy.

One would assume in a process of abstract reasoning that once an economy has reached a very high and elaborate stage of economic development the demand for employment would level off. It would appear that when high standards in the supply of material goods and of services have been reached, people would become satisfied with them so that after a long period of progressive improvements in the standards of living, stretching out over several generations, there would emerge a new traditionalism dedicated to the preservation of the material status quo rather than to its continued change.

At first sight this decline of man-hours of employment seems to take place in highly advanced systems. While the establishment of a normal work week is an indispensable step within an overall structure of economic development, one notable by-product of technological advance is the sharp reduction in the hours underlying the definition of such a maximum work week. Prior to World War I working hours in American industry were in excess of fifty per week; in the 1920's this was reduced to forty-eight hours. In the depression period of the 1930's the work week dropped below forty hours in manufacturing. After World War II, the actual work week was longer, and especially in the 1960's exceeded the forty-hour normal work week by 10 percent in the manufacturing industries. Outside the United States most advanced countries adhered to the forty-eight hour week for a much longer period of time. But as technological advances gained momentum, drastic cuts in the average work week were made in Western Europe as well as in the Soviet Union. However, it would be wrong to interpret this shortening of the normal work week as tantamount to a decline in the demand for employment. Actually it is one outstanding characteristic of economic advance that labor-force participation increases especially in the field of female and part-time employment as output, income, and general levels of prosperity improve. In the United States, labor force participation of white females increased from 30.6 percent in 1948 to 35.9 percent in 1966. This means that as the income and the standard of living of family units increases, advertising and other influences bring into view even higher levels of consumption, including housing, travel, and recreation. This leads to the desire to augment family income which in turn causes more people to participate in the labor force. The shortening of the work week due to increasing labor productivity also provides opportunities for multiple job holding. As is the case with the increasing labor-force participation of women in the United States, the holding of more than one job is not so much dictated by the necessity to earn a basic income for the family but rather by the desire to increase the amount of spending so that the family can share rising levels of prosperity.

There is, however, one oddity in the statistics of labor-force participation which in themselves are a reflection of economic development under conditions of factor transformation. Labor-force participation of single males in the 14–24 age group was far higher in the United States in 1949 than it was in 1963.* In 1949, 45.3 percent of the males 14–19 were participating in the labor force; in 1963, this percentage had gone down to 31.7. In the 20–24 age group the decline was of course less but yet amounted to about 5 percent. Due to this sharp decline of labor-force participation in the youngest age groups, there was a slight overall decline in male labor force attachment. This, however, was overbalanced by the substantial increase in the labor-force participation of women. The drop in juvenile labor-force participation is the reverse of the higher educational achievements that are required in advanced development situations. Terminal degrees of secondary and higher school systems become almost indispensable requirements for entry into the employment structure. The demand for unskilled and undereducated people which was very strong in earlier phases of economic development begins to drop drastically as an advanced system changes from a predominantly blue-collar to a white-collar economy. But this in turn increases the demand for employment. Parents must earn a family income which will be sufficient to provide for the higher education of their children. Hence we see here a continuous escalation of educational requirements on the one side and rising income requirements, which can only be met by gainful employment on the other.

The analysis of labor-force participation and rising educational preconditions for obtaining employment has given us insight into the open-endedness of economic development which does not permit of a leveling off even if a very high plateau of affluence has been reached. There are other reasons which compel a highly advanced system to push ahead regardless of the great abundance already obtained in a previous stage. As factor transformation continues and requires the installation of costly but also highly productive equipment, the apparatus makes full utilization at all times necessary in order to repay the investment and guarantee a further profitable use. Continuous production systems, hitherto confined to such operations as basic steel production, are now introduced in the use of computers. Their employment around the clock is the only way in

*Information on labor-force participation based on *Manpower Report of the President,* 1964, Table B-2.

which they can be utilized at maximum levels of return on the investment. Hence data gathering and processing must be brought up to the level at which this high rate of computer utilization becomes feasible. Although computers replace routine clerical jobs, they also generate somewhat more advanced types of employment dedicated to programming and evaluating of computerized materials. In the late 1960's there was no evidence that the demand for the more qualified clerical and statistical workers would decline. Indications are that it will continue, so that the transition from mechanization to automation could be carried out without a sharp decline in the aggregate demand for labor.

In advanced economies dynamic forces are in operation which require a continuous expansion of output to maintain high levels of employment as productivity continues to increase. It is this basic structure that leads to a continuous redesigning and restyling of products, to the introduction of technical changes and innovations. Everything is oriented toward the generation of rapid processes of obsolescence. Even in construction the rate at which buildings are being torn down and replaced has speeded up considerably as compared to earlier times. Improvement in public services and roads are also carried out on a continuous basis. All this seems to put a rather firm floor under the total structure of employment. Projections of employment in the American economy by 1975 carried out under the optimistic assumption that by that time a "no-war" economy would have settled down in the United States indicate a higher rate of unemployment than prevailed at the heights of the Vietnamese war but still substantially lower than during the "best" year of the Great Depression which was in 1937.* At that time unemployment still was almost 15 percent of the labor force. Projected unemployment by 1975 would be far below this figure, although more than double the average unemployment of the early 1960's.

This economic advance requires a constantly increasing rate of growth of the gross national product in real terms. There must be more consumer spending and more private and public investment each year in order to sustain the forward push of the system. By the same token a standstill or even a decline in the gross national product would bring about a substantial drop in employment. While during the first stage of such a retrogression employment of blue-collar workers would fall much faster than that of nonproduction workers, the latter would also be adversely affected if the economy cannot resume its advance within a comparatively short period.

*Senior Economic Research Project No. 10, Fordham University, 1968.

To sum up: economic development is an all-pervasive aspect. It is necessary to maintain equilibrium even in highly advanced systems. In emerging economies economic development must be pushed forward in order to overcome population pressures and improve the material well-being of people. Without it major parts of the world would encounter a constantly aggravating crisis that would become unmanageable before the end of the twentieth century. Highly advanced countries must continue their upward push in order to avoid a condition of high-level stagnation which, if permitted to last for any length of time, would make the complex structure of such economies increasingly topheavy and would threaten them with decline and deterioration. As seen from the perspective of the 1960's, advanced economies have succeeded far better than emerging countries to realize their development requirements. This has led to the maintenance if not the widening of the gap between developing and developed countries. Such a condition is fraught with danger. We will discuss this paradox of economic development in the next section.

THE CONTINUING GAP

Compared to former periods of economic history, the overall rate of growth in the last third of the century seems to be very impressive. This progressive aspect of the current economic situation must, however, be seen in the context of the great pressures which emanate from rising numbers of people, new production methods and systems, and the greater awareness of people throughout the world of the promises and real possibilities of social and economic improvement. Seen in this perspective, the fact that, relatively speaking, the gap between highly advanced and developing countries has not been narrowed but actually seems to widen is disturbing.

A comparison of annual growth rates of advanced and of developing countries for the years 1963–66 shows that the rate of economic development as expressed in the gross domestic product at constant prices rose faster in advanced countries than in developing countries. If we consider also the fact that population rose much faster in emerging economies than in developed market economies, the disparity between these two groups of systems is shown in its true proportions. The table reproduced below combines information gathered from World Economic Survey 1966 of the United Nations. It shows changes in the GNP and in the population. It should be noted that the two first groups of this table, developed market

Annual Growth Rate of GNP and Population,* 1965–66
(Percentage change from preceding year)

	Developed Market Economies†	Centrally Planned Economies‡	Developing Countries§
Gross domestic product at constant prices	5	7	3
Industrial production....	7	8	8
Agricultural production ..	5	9	−1
Population..........	1.3	1.8	2.6

Sources: World Economic Survey, 1966, United Nations New York 1967, p. 118, *Demographic Yearbook, 1966,* United Nations, New York 1967, pp. 95, 120–131.

**World Economic Survey*, 1966, United Nations, 1967.

†North America, Western Europe, Australia, Japan, New Zealand, and South Africa.

‡Eastern Europe (other than Yugoslavia) and Soviet Union.

§Latin America and the Caribbean, Africa (other than South Africa), Asia (other than mainland China, Cyprus, Japan, Mongolia, North Korea, North Vietnam, and Turkey).

economies and centrally planned economies by and large represent highly advanced systems. The developed market economies are led by the United States, which has the greatest industrial system of the world. The centrally planned economies are led by the Soviet Union, which ranks second among the industrial nations. Other Eastern European nations with a high degree of industrialization are Eastern Germany and Czechoslovakia. It should be noted that mainland China is not listed in any category of this United Nations survey. While the rate of increase in industrial production was somewhat higher in centrally planned and in developing economies than in developed market economies, it must be borne in mind that these slightly higher rates of growth are the inevitable result of the much lower base to which rates of change are being applied. They are not indicative of any discernible trend of the developing countries to close the gap. In fact, the hopes at one time entertained by Soviet leaders of drawing even and then surpassing the American economy by the 1970's have been proven to be unfounded.

The period 1965–66 showed a particularly disturbing trend in agricultural production in developing countries.

While output in farming is subject to noneconomic factors such as weather conditions, the rate of growth of agricultural production in the two preceding years, 2 percent in 1964 and 1 percent in 1965, were below the annual rate of population growth in these developing countries. As a result of this condition and also of the low base of industrial output, personal consumption expenditures in developing countries in 1965 and

1966 rose at substantially lower rates than similar consumption expenditures in advanced countries both of the market economy and centrally planned economy types. In fact, in the latter group the increase in personal consumption expenditures was very high, 9 percent in 1965 and 8 percent in 1966 as compared to 5 percent for each of these two years in market economies and 3 percent in developing countries.*

The steep increases in consumption expenditures in centrally planned economies is the result of the recent rearrangement of priorities in growth targets especially in the Soviet Union. Greater emphasis is being placed on the expansion of consumer goods industries and of services. This has led to a substantial improvement in the standards of living, especially in such basic aspects as nutrition, housing, and clothing of the average Soviet family. Nevertheless these living standards are still lower than those of Western Europe and of the United States. But there is no doubt that as between advanced market and advanced centrally planned economies, the gap, though continuing for the foreseeable future, is narrowing while it is actually widening as between industrialized countries, no matter what their internal economic structure may be, and emerging countries. On a global basis, development policies and economic aid must be designed to narrow the gap between advanced and emergent countries. Unless the "gap paradox" can be eliminated, international instability is bound to increase beyond its already dangerous levels.

*World Economic Survey, 1966, Table 8, United Nations, 1967, p. 124.

chapter **5**

Agricultural Development Under Communism: A Case Study of Scenarios 1 and 3

Development of the farm sector above and beyond traditional low levels of output is one of the bases of economic growth. We have seen that this requires an increase in agrucultural productivity. Eventually this leads to an actual decline in the number of people engaged in agriculture. In fact this drop in the number of people engaged in agriculture can assume such proportions that an attempt has to be made to prevent large-scale dislocation of rural populations which begin to overcrowd cities. Eventually production and employment goals must be reconciled to achieve a new optimum relation between output and employment in agriculture. This is particularly true of systems in which full industrialization is not feasible.

Under Soviet communism this inherent priority on the upbuilding of agriculture was disregarded. There was a great need to push ahead with the development of industry. In Communist China the emphasis of development was on agriculture. In the Soviet Union we find the classical case of Scenario 3 with its pattern of unbalanced growth due to its concentration on heavy industry. In China there is a greater approximation to Scenario 1, especially in the clearly discernible desire of planners to maintain a high rate of employment in the farm sector. We will take up these two cases separately.

THE DEVELOPMENT OF SOVIET AGRICULTURE

Soviet economists will not deny that agriculture has lagged far behind industry in the first fifty years of the Communist regime. This was due to two factors basically independent from each other but which combined to bring about first a period of actual retrogression in agricultural output during the 1930's and later a considerable retardation of growth. The first factor is located in the ineptitude shown by Communists in the formulation and the carrying out of collective systems of agricultural development. Even more important is the second factor which is based on the priority pattern characteristic of Scenario 3 as outlined in Chapter 3.

When the Communists took over during World War I in Russia there had been only a beginning in the build-up of heavy industry. Light industry was also of modest capacity. In the Czarist days Russia had been able to achieve a favorable balance of trade by exporting of agricultural products, especially grains used for animal fodder, timber, and furs. With the surpluses developing from these sales abroad, high-priced consumer goods could be imported. They served the needs of the small group of well-to-do people in old Russia. In view of this state of development at the onset of the Communist system, socialization through the expropriation of capitalist industry, trade, and financial institutions was hardly sufficient to inaugurate that transition from capitalism to socialism which had been visualized by nineteenth century socialist writers. Socialization in Russia did not mean primarily a transformation of private industrial property into a system of social ownership. It rather meant the deliberate creation of new industries under the form of enterprises owned by the state representing in theory the public or society.

Before this building up could get underway, Lenin had to permit a partial and temporary return to capitalism under the name of New Economic Policy (NEP) which extended from 1921 to 1928. In this short period private initiative and operations in the agricultural and in the trade sectors of the system had been able to move the Russian economy from dead center at least back to that level of activity which had prevailed in Russia in 1913. In that year, steel output was about four million tons. Generally in the 1920's standards of living of those not subject to expropriation of their enterprises, estates, and bank accounts had improved gradually. With the return of a modest degree of prosperity, the Communist leaders felt that the time had come to end the NEP and lay the foundations of socialism. These development plans in the form of Five-Year Plans are the most outstanding examples of unbalanced growth. Great priority was given to the development of heavy industries, such as iron and steel and machinery, to the expansion of transportation systems and the development of energy resources on a vast scale. The emphasis on heavy industry was increased by the decision of the Communist leaders to reorganize and strengthen the Red Army as one response to the alleged "capitalistic encirclement." There is no doubt that this priority did pay off in World War II.

The Scenario 3 situation under which the Soviet Union has been operating for so long meant that only limited resources of capital could be made available for enlargement of consumer-goods output, building construction, and agricultural development. In fact this low priority of the farm sector forced Soviet agriculture to retain a labor-intensive pattern resulting in low yields per acre. This imbalance in economic development was aggravated by the infusion of political and ideological considerations into the organizational design of agricultural production units. Actually Communist systems have differed and continue to differ on specific policies dealing with their agricultural sector. We will accordingly consider separately the Russian and the Chinese approach to agricultural development.

Prior to the Bolshevik revolution the vast majority of the rural population in Russia consisted of sharecroppers and agricultural laborers. While there was also a number of prosperous farmers, a vast proportion of the agricultural area was in the hands of wealthy landowners or proprietors. It is significant that when Lenin started his final push for power in 1917, far from promising abolition of private property of land he actually proposed an increase in the number of property holdings by redistributing the big estates among the land poor or landless peasantry.

This actually was the policy carried out after the takeover of the Communists. The big landowners were expropriated without compensation and the land was doled out in small parcels to the village population. It should be noted that the same procedures were carried out by other Communist regimes in Europe after World War II wherever there had been a survival of large-scale land ownership. Although the average size of the land handed over to peasants was rather small, there was a noticeable revival of agricultural output in Russia especially during the period of the new economic policy. Furthermore, a new middle class of farmers, the so-called *kulaki* or kulaks, gained additional strength. If we take into consideration that in the first ten years of the Communist regime there was no decline in the rural population—it still was over 80 percent—it is easy to see why for purely political considerations the Communist party decided to bring about in a short period of time a complete structural change in the agricultural sector. Had such a policy not been enacted, the increasing prosperity of individual farmers could not fail to shift the balance of power in Russia from the Communists to the property-owning farm population. This is an explanation why forcible farm collectivization did take place in the Soviet Union. It is no apology for the brutal methods used in carrying out these policy objectives.

The first Five-Year Plan which instituted the priority for heavy industry also provided for the collectivization of agriculture. The farmers were compelled to pool all their plots into the *Kolkhoz,* which was legally construed as agricultural cooperative. In addition to these collective farms, *state farms* covering large areas were set up. The difference in the structure and operation of these two types of agricultural production units was considerable. The state farms directly owned by the government represent a type of industrial operation in agriculture specializing in large-scale output of grains and other staples. These production units employ agricultural laborers receiving a straight wage.

We have already seen in Chapter 4 that over the years the number of collective farms have been cut down drastically as their average size increased. There is a long-range goal in the Soviet Union of replacing them completely with state farms. At this point of our discussion we are, however, concerned with the institutional factor of collective farms as it existed under Scenario 3 conditions in which the greatest emphasis was placed on heavy industry and the creation of social overhead capital.

There is a strange similarity between the work arrangements of the collective farm and of the feudal estate. In both cases all those living on the land were obligated to render a stated amount of labor services. On the Kolkhoz the average labor obligation was defined as amounting to 200 days a year. If this does not seem to be a very large commitment let us remember that winters in Russia are long and the planting and growing seasons are necessarily short. Like the situation in early feudalism, collective farms had to make deliveries in kind to government collecting agencies. Some taxes also had to be paid in kind and a similar system prevailed for rental payments to the motor tractor stations. The collective farm workers also received part of their payment in kind. Additional compensation depended on the actual number of work days performed by individual members of the collective. The transition from individual farm operations to collective also forced the surrender of all livestock to the Kolkhoz. There was widespread resistance and many farmers slaughtered their cattle rather than turn it over to the new collective. It took the Soviet Union many years to make up for the tremendous losses in livestock brought about by the way in which forcible collectivization was carried out in the early 1930's.

In fact the collective farm as originally constituted represented a retrogressive development in agriculture. It was highly labor-intensive but did not create incentives for efficient work. This arrangement was not the result of a deliberate policy to establish optimum levels of employment opportunities for a rural population which otherwise would remain unemployed. Rather it was a product of the desire to eliminate as soon as possible private property on land and individual operations of small farms. To achieve these political objectives and to concentrate all resources on priority industrial investments, agricultural development was permitted to lag far behind economic growth and even a rising population. Per capita food consumption in the 1930's dropped below pre-World War I levels. Even before World War II Stalin had to make a major concession in order to stop further deterioration of farm production. Collective farmers were permitted to work for their own account so-called *individual garden plots*. Soon many members of the collective began to spend most of their time for the intensive utilization of these small strips of land. As a result a great proportion of the supply of vegetables, fruits, and some dairy products of the Soviet Union was produced on these individual plots.

Experience in other Communist countries permits almost the establishment of an "economic law" of agricultural development under socialism: transition from individual to collective farm operation inevitably leads to a decline in farm output. This is particularly true whenever socialization of agriculture occurs in a Scenario 3 setting in which few resources are available for the creation of additional farm equipment.

Eventually this first and painful phase of agricultural development under socialism comes to an end. The termination of this first period can assume different forms. In Poland and Yugoslavia collectivization drives yielded to the desire of farmers for individual farm operations. In the Soviet Union itself, beginning in the 1950's, basic structural changes in the original design of the collective farm were introduced. Incentives were increased in a number of ways. The government discarded the long-standing policy of accepting one part of the output of the collective farm in kind and paying a very low price for the remainder of the compulsory deliveries. Now all products of the collective farms are turned over to the government against payment of a substantially higher price. Accordingly the revenue of the collective farm and of the individual worker was increased considerably. Up until recently the average earnings per month of collective farmers amounted only to 29 rubles or $32. Beginning in 1967 collective farmers received a guaranteed monthly wage of about 54 rubles. Similar improvements were made in the compensation of wage earners on the state farms.

Over the years the individual garden plots had come under frequent attack in the Communist press because they seemed to be a capitalistic survival. On the other hand, as we have already seen, without these private efforts of collective farmers the diet of the Soviet citizen would have been even more deficient in fruits and vegetables than it actually was. The new policy of increasing revenue and output of collective farms and creating income incentives to its members has not resulted in a ban on the individual plots. The new system of improved compensation of collective farms still provides for some allocation in kind of grain and hay. They can be used to feed the livestock held by individual farm families. It is expected that this measure will actually increase the output of meat, milk, and eggs. Individual plots will continue, as will the produce markets in Russian cities where farmers from the countryside sell vegetables, fruits, and dairy products. To demonstrate the scope of these activities the story of some grape growers from Soviet Georgia can serve as an illustration. Taking advantage of the extremely low passenger fares on Soviet planes, some farmers from Soviet Georgia were able to fly to Moscow, sell their fresh grapes on the free-produce market and fly back home with a substantial profit. It should be noted that such economic initiative is not illegal in the Soviet Union as long as it does not involve the employment of wage earners for the private advantage of such a business operation.

In 1967 basic changes were also introduced in the state farms. Many had been operating with a deficit due to the very low prices paid by the government agencies. For instance, in 1965 the government had to put up more than a billion rubles to cover the deficits that had accrued in the 12,000 state farms. A 10 percent increase in prices was granted. This brought about an equalization of prices received by collective farms after the initial boost of prices granted to them and the prices of the products of these state farms. On an experimental basis a new profit incentive system in which managers and workers shared was introduced in 400 state farms. This scheme is similar to the one already in operation in a number of manufacturing industries in the Soviet Union, especially in the consumer-goods sector. According to this plan, premiums are paid whenever the operation shows higher profits as a result of a lowering of production costs, especially through higher output per man-hour and a decline in unit labor requirements.

While this productivity bonus will apply only to those state farms included in this profit-sharing experiment, all workers on state farms have been placed on a monthly wage at the same levels prevailing now in collective farms.

In the initial stages of agricultural development in the Soviet Union, the main emphasis was placed on a change in the institutional structure of the farm sector. Attempts to improve farm output were confined to the introduction of motor tractors. This was not sufficient to bring about a substantial increase in output after the great decline which accompanied the period of collectivization. After World War II the pattern of unbalanced growth following the Scenario 3 was maintained for a considerable time. Only after 1960 do we find attempts to increase agricultural productivity by allocating more resources for the creation of industrial facilities capable of lifting levels of farm production. Up to that point chemical fertilizers had been used in the Soviet Union only to a limited degree. Attempts to order complete chemical plants designed for the production of fertilizers from the West—especially Germany—failed. Eventually a crash program was introduced to build up the chemical industry in the Soviet Union.

In the late 1960's the impact of all the measures described in this section became noticeable. Farm output began to increase after the disastrous crop failures of the early 1960's. Studies carried out by Soviet sociologists on a number of farms showed a substantial increase in the income of farm families. This increase was due not only to the higher wage guarantees but also to an intensification of work on the private plots. Nevertheless the opportunities in the industrial sector continued to attract young people from farm areas. To counteract this flight from the open countryside, permission was given to collective farms to establish producer cooperatives on collective farms in the area of light industries. The intention is to gear the output of such cooperative enterprises to the needs of local consumer goods markets.

By and large the agricultural development under Soviet communism seems on the way of recovering from the dislocations of forcible collectivization, from the disabilities of having to operate in a low-priority sector of the unbalanced growth model of the Soviet economy, gradually reaching the state of accelerated growth in output as well as in productivity. The latter fact is clearly demonstrated by the decline in the number of farm workers. Within the short period between 1958 and 1965 their number fell from 25 million to 18 million. While this is still an extremely large proportion of the total labor force as compared to the United States, this decrease in farm labor indicates that at long last productivity in Soviet agriculture is rising.

It should be noted that the retention of a highly labor-intensive pattern of farm operation in the Soviet Union was not based on the desire to combine output goals with maximum employment targets. The rapid growth of the industrial sector in the Soviet Union generated a general condition of labor shortages in the nonagricultural industries. The low productivity was primarily the result of the concentration on industrial investment while most of the labor force was coming from the countryside and had no experience in the disciplines and routines of factory employment. In agriculture productivity remained very low over decades because the system of compensation of the farm population did not provide reward for higher individual efforts. But in the fifty years of Soviet communism a restructuring of the labor force has taken place. Today the farm workers and collective farmers in the Soviet Union constitute less than 20 percent of the total labor force which exceeds 100 million. It follows that the Communist leaders fear that a majority of the farm population would be a threat to socialization if permitted to stay outside the socialist sector and to work exclusively on their own land has largely dissipated. The pattern of agriculture which emerges in the Soviet Union shows a trend toward industrialization of farming in the form of huge state farms on the one hand and a toleration of specialized individual farm activity on so-called garden plots on the other. As productivity in agriculture continues to rise, there will be a further reduction in the farm labor force. At the same time the quality and the variety of food production will continue to improve.

AGRICULTURE UNDER CHINESE COMMUNISM

The development of Chinese communism has taken from the very beginning an altogether different course than that of the Russian precedent. While many aspects of Chinese communism, for instance, the great unrest brought about by the "cultural revolution" and the personality cult of Mao Tse-tung in the 1960's cannot be explained without reference to deep-rooted aspects of Chinese society going back almost three thousand years, the pattern of development of the economic system is, strangely enough, more "normal" than the forced industrialization to which the Russian people were exposed with so many hardships in the first fifty years of Soviet communism.*

While China had been brought rather forcefully into international trade and commerce with the opening up of such treaty ports as Shanghai

---

*Fei and Chiang in their study quoted in Annotation 1, Chapter I, classify China as a case of MSD—maximum speed development. This seems doubtful. Chinese communism operates largely with more intensive and effective utilization of labor. Unlike the Soviet Union, Communist China has not given top priority to the build-up of heavy industry. Rather it stresses light industry and the development of agriculture. The Chinese crash program in nuclear weapons and delivery systems is not characteristic of the overall pattern of Chinese development.

late in the nineteenth century, the country was even less developed industrially after World War II than Russia had been prior to World War I. A
clear evidence of this lag was the goal pronounced by Communist leaders
in China in 1958, to overtake Great Britain in industrial production within
fifteen years. This was a modest aim if we consider the fact that even then
the Chinese population was at least twelve times that of Great Britain and
was rapidly approaching the 700-million mark.

In sharp contrast to the priority system embodied in the Five-Year
Plans of the Soviet Union, Mao stressed the importance of agriculture.
However, the Chinese are confronted in this area with formidable challenges. While the population of China is roughly 20 percent of the total
world population, the country has at its disposal only about 8 percent of
the arable land of the planet. Over a long period of time peasant families in
China had tilled the soil on very small plots, averaging no more than three
acres. They engaged in intensive agriculture, using a great deal of manure
as fertilizer generally ekeing out a very modest income. The "landlords"
which came under immediate attack after the Communists took over in
1949 were not manorial lords in a feudal way as they existed in Europe
and also in Japan. Rather they were middle-class people who had managed
primarily through business transactions in the cities to accumulate larger
tracts of land in the countryside. Now as in most Communist revolutions
these landlords were expropriated, often after they had been compelled to
confess publicly the "sins" they had committed in the operation of their
land.

In view of the fact that Chinese farmers had worked on their own
small plots, there was not a great redistribution of land as it had occurred
immediately after the Communist revolution in Russia. Rather there was a
progressive collectivization of the small farms—that is to say, their combination into larger productive cooperatives which also would acquire lands
taken away from the landlord. In the short period between 1949 and
1953, 71 percent of the peasants had been put into these collectives. Only
29 percent of the peasants were still outside the system and were classified
as "poor farmers" although they were hardly worse off than the farmers
already in the collective farms. In the years that followed, most of these
poor farmers were also included into the ranks of the agricultural collectives. By 1958 there were no less than 750 thousand collective farms
comprising 123 million farm families. It should be noted that these figures
indicate the continuing very high percentage of the rural population in
Chinese society. The main purpose of the collectivization of farms had
been the increase of the size of the farm units, the beginning of greater

specialization of farm production, and the attempt to utilize agricultural manpower more effectively.

It was at this point in the development of agriculture under Chinese Communism that a dramatic change was carried out with great speed. In the "Great Leap Forward" the comparatively small collective farms were to be grouped into 26,500 "communes." These communes were conceived not only as large-scale agricultural production units; they were also intended to develop industrial operations and make a contribution to a dramatic increase in industrial output while at the same time establishing a pattern of industrial decentralization. Furthermore, the original design for the communes provided for communal living in dormitories, common eating facilities, and the setting up of crèches or day nurseries to enable women to become more fully involved in the labor force.

Actually this concept of an agricultural-industrial commune was not of Chinese origin at all. It was advocated almost in the same way in the 1830's by Charles Fourier in France who for a time found many adherents even in the United States, for instance in the famous Brook Farm at West Roxbury, Mass. Just as Karl Marx and Friedrich Engels denounced Fourier's plans as utopian, Soviet theorists a hundred years later took immediate issue with the Chinese communes. One charge was that this policy tried to disrupt the "dialectical sequence" in the development toward socialism. According to the doctrine of historical materialism, it is not possible to skip any of the "inevitable phases" of the transformation of the economic system.

The original scheme of the Chinese communes did not survive for long. There was great resistance on the part of the farmers against the breaking up of traditional forms of family living. There was also resentment against the almost military organization of farm work. It included reveille, march in formation to assigned work areas, constant supervision, and exposure to propaganda broadcasts.

The attempt to enforce a tremendous increase in the output of pig iron by the installation of primitive, preindustrial blast furnaces in many areas where communes were located near iron ore deposits was also a complete failure. While a great deal of pig iron was produced in this primitive fashion it proved totally unsuitable when attempts were made to transform it into steel or use it for other purposes of manufacturing. This ill-conceived attempt at rapid expansion of iron and steel production had to be abandoned after a short period of time.

Soon Communist authorities had to give up the communal life pattern on the communes. As in the Soviet Union farmers again were permitted to work individual plots and sell their produce on nearby free markets. Nevertheless the communes as such were continued and there was no return to the much smaller agricultural collectives of the first phase of Chinese communism. In fact, the basic idea of combining in one commune agricultural and industrial activities was retained even after the early attempts of total communal living had been abandoned. In 1966 a new type of state farm was established in Kiangsi Province in which more than 11,000 people were engaged in such different activities as grain production, the raising of silkworms, and silk weaving. Like in the Soviet Union in the 1930's the Chinese in the 1960's would display model communes to foreign visitors and correspondents. One just outside Peking had 40,000 members in 1965. There were 40 medical doctors and 24 primary and secondary schools. The main product of this farm was vegetables. However, there are also piggeries and orchards. Six percent of the total land is held in private plots which, however, are big enough to raise enough for the family to sell some of their produce on the free market. This showplace was started in 1958 at the time of the communization drive. While it is not typical of the average commune in China it may be representative of what the Chinese Communists have in mind for the agricultural sector. In 1959 an Indian social scientist described another model farm called "the commune of the sixteen guarantees." In a report reprinted in the *New York Times* on February 21, 1959, some of the guarantees comprised transportation to place of work, maternity benefits, free old-age care, funeral and burial, free education, and small marriage grants. There was even reference to twelve free haircuts and twenty free bath tickets a year.

We have seen earlier in this section that the Chinese Communist approach to economic development gave priority to agriculture. This was also clearly indicated in the output goals for grain production as they were formulated at the time when the communes were being set up in great haste. There was an output goal of 250 million tons for 1962 and for a virtual doubling of this quantity by 1967. It was hoped that collectivization and the extension of the arable area by the cultivation of virgin land would make possible this accelerated rise in grain output. These programs were to be accompanied by flood-control measures, and by improvements in drainage and irrigation. In this connection it must be stressed that traditionally agricultural operations in China have been impaired frequently by floods, droughts, and hurricanes. In the early 1960's a number of poor crop years resulted in a catastrophic decline in agricultural output. The Chinese were compelled to contract for large-scale imports of grains, especially from Canada. In the initial years of the communes malnutrition was widespread and could be found even among the armed forces.

The extent of the failure to develop agriculture in China can be seen easily by comparing grain output in 1957, just before the introduction of the communes and in 1967, ten years later. In 1957 grain output amounted to 184 million tons; in 1967 it was 187 million tons. This was hailed as the second-best output in Chinese agricultural history, but actually it was about the same quantity that had been produced ten years earlier. Taking ten million as the lowest estimate of an annual increase in population in Communist China, this would mean that grain output remained the same while the population increased by 100 million (or one-half the total population of the United States). Of course, grain output is only one success indicator of agricultural development. Actually the realized grain crop enabled the Chinese to cut back their grain imports to 3.4 million metric tons in 1968. Observers agree that there have been no regional hunger epidemics in China as they were occurring occasionally throughout the history of that country especially because poor transportation made it impossible to ship surpluses from one area to places where crops had failed and people were starving.

Actually the Chinese Communists experienced the same disruption and decline of agricultural production in the years following the setting up of the communes that the Russian Communists suffered in the early 1930's. There is no doubt that in these two cases of agricultural development under communism the major mistake that was being made was in the matter of timing. In both cases political and ideological considerations caused the leadership to plunge into a rush toward collectivization. They were afraid of the threat to the Communist structure inherent in a free peasantry even if the average size of individual farms was extremely small.

If we consider the agricultural development in advanced industrial countries such as the United States, we must conclude that in the long run modern agricultural technology is incompatible with small, individually operated farm plots as they existed in China for a long time and also in the Soviet Union in the years immediately following the dividing up of the huge landed estates. Furthermore, strictly on theoretical grounds of manpower use it could be argued that a retention of a pattern of many millions of midget farms represents a considerable waste in terms of manpower. The design of the Chinese communes has clearly the purpose to make more women available for work outside the burdensome but limited field of subsistence farming. Another justification for the concept of the commune would be the realization of the old, nineteenth-century idea of combining in huge settlements agricultural and industrial activities.

As far as Communist China is concerned, this would be consistent with the Scenario 1 pattern of economic development which comes closer to their priorities system than the Soviet Five-Year Plans which are out-standing models of unbalanced growth systems. Agricultural-industrial units could also be considered as one way of avoiding the type of disloca-tion of rural populations which can lead to the paradoxical situation which we have discussed in the first section of Chapter 4. Under a development pattern following the sectoral growth rather than the factor-transformation method of economic development agricultural output could rise eventually even in a commune setting without producing at the same time an agricultural surplus population.

In an overall comparison between Communist methods of agricultural development and Western practices, it is obvious that all success indicators, such as increase in output, improvements in quality and variety, efficient use of agricultural labor, the Communists present a picture of backward-ness and inefficiency. However, it would be an oversimplification to trace this advantage of Western countries to a contrast between individual ownership and collective operations of family units. Actually in the United States the corporate form of farm enterprises has made very great strides, and generally speaking the steady rise in output and productivity in the agricultural sector of the United States has been accompanied by an extremely sharp drop in individually owned farm units. The conclusion suggests itself that while Western agriculture was undergoing a rapid process of factor transformation it was not at the same time subjected to ideology-induced campaigns to transform in a short period private owner-ship into collective structures in farming. Furthermore both in the United States and Europe, at least until the mid-1960's, a very substantial techno-logical labor displacement in the farm sector could be absorbed in the rapidly expanding nonagricultural industries. But the appearance of large areas of chronic unemployment in urban centers of the United States in the latter part of the decade was indicative of the fact that the problem of reconciling the goals of agricultural development with its labor displace-ment and of maintaining full employment for the system as a whole had not yet been mastered.

chapter 6

Two Cases of Factor Transformation: Germany and Japan

It is a somewhat ironic fact that West Germany and Japan, the two major countries that suffered a crushing defeat in World War II, were able in a comparatively short period not only to reach prewar levels of per capita income and output but to continue economic development at unusually high rates of growth. Prior to the World War II undivided Germany was second only to the United States in terms of industrial output. After World War II the Soviet Union replaced Germany in this ranking. West Germany has a precarious hold on the third place, with Japan very close behind. However, if East Germany—in the late 1960's still under a Stalinist type of government—were added to West Germany, all of Germany would be assured of retaining third place for a considerable period of time. Actually in this ranking of industrial nations East Germany has tenth place.

The significance of these rankings should not be overrated. The assumption that bigness, as such, and mere quantity of output are indicative of an efficient and socially satisfactory operation of the system cannot be accepted without thorough investigation. However, from the viewpoint of a study of economic development the spectacular success of Germany as well as Japan is of great interest. Compared with the base period of 1958, industrial production rose to 169 in 1966 in West Germany; in Japan it reached the extremely high level of 325 during the same year. Even if we take into account that the rate of growth indicated in such indices appears higher when the performance at the base period was lower, there is no denying the fact that these rates of growth are exceptional. These success indicators of West Germany and Japan are also remarkable because neither country was attempting to carry out basic structural changes in underlying social conditions, especially the system of private ownership of means of production and business. Both countries share the tendency toward concentration of basic manufacturing and financial activities in huge business corporations. They also have similarities so far as attitudes of the labor force are concerned which in these countries are conducive to sustained effort and avoidance of protracted industrial conflicts. But while in these two countries basic social institutions did not experience revolutionary changes, the economic system was subjected to radical factor transformation. These altered conditions require our detailed attention. Although there are similarities between West Germany and Japan as they have been outlined here, the historical and institutional setting at the zero point after World War II was so different that we will now discuss the case of Germany and Japan separately.

THE SO-CALLED GERMAN ECONOMIC MIRACLE

It was mentioned in the opening chapter that there is frequently an intrusion of ideology into economic analysis and that the time has come to engage in a demythologization of economics. We will engage in this task while tracing the road of economic development in West Germany after World War II. When it became clear in the early 1950's that recovery in West Germany was lifting this recently defeated country far above levels of prosperity experienced before, even professional economists in the United States began to attribute this "miracle" to the speedy introduction of a free market and free-enterprise system in Germany after the war. This was sometimes used to engage in invidious comparisons between the "capitalist" performance of West Germany and the "socialist" management of the economy in the United Kingdom under the leadership of the British Labor Party. As we will see shortly, the free-enterprise system in Germany operated during this whole period of speedy recovery under conditions of large-scale government intervention in many vital sectors of the economy, so that the institutional pattern was quite different from the model of a free-market system. However, it is necessary to define in greater detail the situation at the postwar zero point.

As the strategic bombing survey conducted after World War II showed clearly, conventional area bombing did not prevent output in Germany from reaching a maximum in 1944. This was achieved through a high degree of decentralization and subcontracting in industrial production and the virtual cessation of output for nondefense purposes. The same survey also demonstrated that heavy production equipment which is anchored in the ground can survive a great deal of nonnuclear aerial bombing. However, when land warfare came to Germany early in 1945, large-scale destruction of economically important facilities occurred. At the end of hositlities no railroad or highway bridge was operative. Water-supply systems functioned with difficulties. At least 25 percent of residential housing had been destroyed to some extent by artillery action in connection with hostilities. On the ground, there was then a virtual stand-still of economic activities, aggravated by the fact that the country was no longer administered by a central government. The Allied Powers had taken its place and the country was carved up into four occupation zones. Inflation originally repressed through stiff price controls started to become manifest. Enormous amounts of old currency had also been paid out to people who had lost their homes as a result of allied bombing. There was a widespread repudiation of this inflated currency and many transactions were made in the form of barter deals. American cigarettes were used as a medium of exchange. While the German government had been disestablished, the laws and regulations dealing with wage and price controls remained intact for the time being.

Actually some of these controls had been in effect long before World War II. Already during the depression starting in 1929, the German government had carried out a deliberate policy of deflation so far as personal income was concerned. When the National Socialists took over they dissolved labor unions, abolished free collective bargaining, and continued the wage freeze. Actually aggregate wages did rise as the war economy got underway due to an upgrading of many workers into higher job classes and overtime pay. Rent control going back to World War I was continued. When the World War II started a very comprehensive system of rationing was put into effect immediately. While there was no change in the property structure of industry, agriculture, and business, the government intervened to an ever greater extent in the economic process by setting up investment priorities. When industry refused to make funds available for the setting up of the Volkswagen Plant, the money was taken out of the vast surpluses of the Nazi Labor Front Organization. Equally a new huge steel combine designed to utilize low-grade iron was set up as a publicly owned corporation because industry assumed, erroneously as it turned out later, that this operation could not be carried out profitably.

It is this type of system which was described as a "command economy." Now for the first three years after V-E Day the command economy was continued. This meant that very little was available in official markets and at controlled prices still quoted in the old prewar and war currency. Black-market operations assumed a vast proportion. While wages continued under the official freeze, employers trying to start up production were forced to make deals with farmers and business firms assuring some supplementary payments in kind to the employees. A great deal of time had to be spent in repairing production facilities. It soon became clear that the inflated currency would be replaced by a new stable medium of exchange. In fact this proved to be easier than in democratic countries which require some sort of parliamentary approval for such a sweeping operation, because in 1948 the Allied Powers were functioning as the government in Germany and were not accountable to elected representatives.

In the period prior to the currency conversion which incidentally was followed immediately by the breakaway from joint Allied control of the Russian-occupied zone in Germany, many producers of consumer goods had been able to resume production at least on a limited scale. However, anticipating the currency reform, they preferred to build up their inventories rather than to make their merchandise available for retail sales. Actually, prior to the introduction of the new currency there was a large-scale sellers' strike in Germany.

In June 1948, the old currency was replaced by the new one on a 10-to-1 basis. This meant a corresponding cut in all money deposits by individuals and business. But because wages and social security benefits had been frozen over so many years, these income shares continued to be paid out on a 1-to-1 basis so that nominally workers received the same amount in the new money that they had obtained in the old currency. Naturally, on the other side of the ledger, the reform brought about a 90 percent cut in public and private indebtedness. Generally this favored property owners and those manufacturers who had stocked up their inventories during the period of inflation.

As currency reform was approaching in West Germany, two schools of thought engaged in a discussion of what to do with the remaining price and wage controls. One group advocated their retention for a transitional period; the other, headed by Professor Erhard who later became Minister of Economics and, for a short period, Chancellor of the Bonn Republic, favored the simultaneous change in currency and abolition of the command economy. This argument won out and the stage was set for the so-called German economic miracle.

In fact, the moment the new currency went into effect hitherto bare shelves and shop windows were filled with merchandise. Food almost immediately became more abundant and black markets disappeared. There was nothing miraculous about this development. All it signified was that the sellers' strike had been terminated. Huge profits could be realized because in terms of the new currency the cost of production of the goods which had been put out in inventory during the preceding period of inflation had been extremely low.

The termination of the command economy was conceived by Dr. Erhard and his advisors—chief among whom was Professor Wilhelm Roepke —as a return to a free-market system. However, this model was somewhat modified by considerations of welfare economics in the sense of such economists as A. C. Pigou. The government expressed concern for the welfare of the lower-income groups. The simple competitive model was expanded into the concept of a *social market economy*. This meant retention for the time being of rent control and a comprehensive revision and eventual upgrading of the German social security system. On the other hand, this concept excluded government participation in the formulation of growth targets even in the modified forms that have been practiced in France since 1946. There was even great reluctance until 1966 to establish in West Germany a body comparable to the Council of Economic Advisors as it exists in the United States since passage of the Employment Act of 1946.

It would be a grave ideological distortion, however, to attribute the high rate of growth of the German economy to the operation of the market forces under conditions of an entirely free and unregulated system. Actually even after the elimination of the command economy the German economic structure continued to be subject to a number of official and voluntary restraints which taken together amounted to a strong intervention by government and organized bodies such as labor unions and farm organizations into the forces of a free market.

This intervention moved in contradictory ways. On the one hand, rent control was continued until the 1960's when the housing shortage had been overcome by high rates of residential construction. On the other hand, high agricultural price levels were assured through protective tariffs until the establishment of the European Common Market created a more uniform price level among the participating countries. The agricultural agreements of the Common Market countries brought German grain prices down somewhat while raising French prices. In the first years after monetary stabilization organized labor in Germany showed great restraint in demanding higher wages. Only about ten years after the start of the new currency was there a great upward push of wages. The low wages prevalent in German industry in that period enabled manufacturing enterprises to accumulate huge internal savings which then could be used for expansion, modernization, and automation. However, in the investment sector government fiscal policies established a framework within which private initiative and managerial skill did find a favorable setting. It is this area which makes a study of German economic development after World War II so interesting.

Large-scale destruction, while creating enormous losses to business and untold hardships to the population, nevertheless opened up vast opportunities and incentives for investment once the causes of the devastation had been eliminated. Under such conditions there was for a considerable period of time an almost unlimited need for investment not only in order to rebuild what has been destroyed but also in virtually all segments of the demand for consumer goods. The problem of reconstruction and of growth, therefore, boiled down to one of finance. Here the Bonn government provided a number of fiscal devices to stimulate investment without impairing private initiative.

In view of the huge devastation of the residential section of German cities reconstruction of housing was of prime importance. For a considerable period of years more than 500,000 dwelling units were built in West Germany. On a population basis this rate was at least twice as high as the annual residential construction in the United States during the same years. Furthermore, about 80 percent of the new housing was carried out under the program of "social building construction." That is, the government would guarantee or grant low interest loans to builders of new houses if they agreed to establish approved ceilings on rents. The capital put up by the builder himself could be written off by means of income tax liability provisions in a short period of time. In addition to this individuals could set aside savings designed to finance private dwellings. Here again substantial tax advantages were granted.

This highly successful development of the residential housing sector in Germany is entirely different in concept from the low-rent housing projects in the United States. The government, apart from the regular supervisory agencies that issue building permits, had nothing to do with the design of housing. While the builders were obligated to accept tenants who had lost their homes as a result of wartime destruction or who had been expelled from areas coming under Communist control, the income ceilings for this type of housing were far higher than the poverty criteria used in the United States. If a comparison is to be made between the United States and West Germany, it should be done only on the level of middle-income housing.

Equally great tax advantages were given to industrial investment. New equipment could be written off in a short period of time. In addition to protecting farm prices, the government, partly with funds accruing within the Common Market settlements, made large credits available for the purchase of modern farm equipment and even modern farm houses.

Like other countries in the West, West Germany benefited greatly from the *Marshall Plan*. The experience in Germany and elsewhere with this type of reconstruction assistance showed the effectiveness of foreign economic aid when it is given to countries temporarily weakened but richly endowed with managerial and engineering skills and high levels of labor productivity. In the initial period of reconstruction West Germany also had the advantage of not having to allocate resources for defense expenditures. At the same time the presence of allied occupation forces and their dependents led to an accumulation of foreign exchange reserves in West Germany.

At first sight the millions of Germans flowing into the western part of the country after their flight or expulsion from Central and Eastern European areas that had come under Communist control seemed to aggravate the problems of reconstruction and development. However, substantial labor shortages soon developed as reconstruction and expansion gained momentum. Now it is clear that the rate of growth of the West German economy could not have been achieved if it had not been for this substantial addition to the labor force. Early in the 1960's even these new arrivals in West Germany were not sufficient to meet the demand for labor. At one point more than a million foreign workers, primarily from Italy, Spain, and Greece, were employed in West Germany.

While the Marshall Plan was the indispensable first move in getting development started, the complex system of controls, tax incentives, and support to agriculture as previously outlined suggest that the development of West Germany at least after 1952 comes close to the "bootstrap model." If we take the year 1938 as a base, industrial production in West Germany in 1947 was only 33 percent. In the years to 1950 it almost tripled and reached 96 percent in 1950. If we take the GNP, again based on 1938 = 100 the GNP in 1961 had already reached the level of 224. At that point the postwar rate of growth of West Germany had by far outstripped that of other Western European countries. In the same year the GNP in the United Kingdom was only 48 percent above the pre-World War II level, France had reached 197 index points in 1961. In the early part of the 1960's this rapid rate of growth continued in Western Germany. Industrial production rose by almost 95 percent between 1954 and 1964. Now this latter phase of economic development in West Germany is due to a large extent to growth induced and promoted by *factor transformation*.

While industrial output in the ten-year period preceding 1964 rose by 95 percent, industrial employment increased only by 29 percent. In fact, in 1962 when output had reached a level of 176 percent employment in industry had risen to 30 percent over 1954. In the next two years output rose by another 19 index points but employment dropped by one point. Furthermore, by 1964 the average work week had dropped 14 index points below 1954.

We encounter here a particularly rapid process of factor transformation which is indicative of the great efforts made by German industry to speed up modernization and automation of production. This high rate of progress in production efficiency in Germany is due to two entirely different sets of circumstances. To some extent the original plan for a deindustrialization of Germany was carried out by the Allies in the years after 1945. Selected plants, especially steelmaking facilities, were dismantled and reinstalled in Allied countries. The Soviet Union was also given some of these facilities dismantled in Western Europe. Now when this original policy was terminated and the production ceilings on the output of heavy industry in Germany were lifted, new equipment was installed which inevitably was technically superior to the installations that had been dismantled. The second reason why automation was introduced on a broad scale was the labor shortage in West Germany. Due to the losses in World War II and the low birth rates in the postwar period, a long-run labor shortage was indicated. Studies carried out by the German Institute for Business Research shows clearly that without automation especially in office operations in banks, insurance companies, and public administration, the great increase in the volume of business could not have been handled because labor shortages would have hindered the rate of growth of going up to the high percentages it obtained in the late 1950's.

While the short-run goal of economic reconstruction immediately after World War II had been the restoration of prewar levels of coal output, great structural changes in the demand for fuels brought about a sharp curtailment in the demand for coal later on. In the 1960's a considerable number of mines were closed down, while those remaining in production were thoroughly modernized. It is characteristic of the high degree of interventionism in the German economy that in recent years the federal government has resorted to a policy of subsidies of the mining industries. As a result, coal production continued at a level in excess of sales possibilities and mountains of coal piled up outside of many coal mines. Nevertheless there was a substantial labor displacement in the mining industry. The widely held opinion that workers who spent a considerable time in coal mining could not be retrained for other types of employment was refuted by the successful transfer of many displaced miners to manufacturing, especially in newly established assembly plants of the automobile industry.

We have seen at the beginning of this section that basically the economy of West Germany continued to operate as a private-enterprise system. Actually a skillful mix of tax incentives granted to private investors contributed greatly to the favorable result of the development drive. However, it is necessary to emphasize that the West German economy does not correspond in any way to the basic model of a free competitive system. This is due to a very high degree of concentration in industry and in banking and to government intervention in the private sector which far exceeds anything known in peacetime American economy.

It is true that the Allied Powers forced two of the largest corporations of the world, the German United Steel Company and the Chemical Trust, into decartelization and insisted on the dissolution of the joint-sales office of the German coal mining industry. These giant enterprises in steel and in chemistry had been created in the 1920's in connection with the structural streamlining procedures carried out at that time under the slogan of economic rationalization. After World War II the firms which originally had merged in the steel and chemical industries were reestablished as independent corporations. However, these units are still huge business enterprises. In banking the German system of large concentrated banks with innumerable branches all over the country continued after the failure of occupation authorities to bring about a greater degree of decentralization. If it was the purpose of Allied economic policies in Germany to induce a shift from monopolistic to free competition in the German economy, it must be said that this has failed to a great extent. In fact, while there was a sustained high level of prosperity in West Germany actually covering (by the late 1960's) a twenty-year period, there were a number of spectacular business failures even of large-scale industrial enterprises. A closer examination of the causes of these failures shows that these businesses ran into trouble precisely because they were old-style free enterprises still operated in a highly personal style by owner-managers. When one of the largest industrial combines in the world, the Krupp Company in Essen, became illiquid, the Bonn government provided sufficient guarantees and the old family-controlled enterprise, which after World War II had refused to resume defense production, was transformed into a corporation.

State intervention in support of the mining industry and occasionally to safeguard an individual business enterprise is not the only deviation in

West Germany from the classical model of a capitalistic private-enterprise system. Much has been made of the "privatization" of the Volkswagen plant. Actually the federal government and the state in which the plant is located have retained 49 percent of the shares. Modeled on the Ford Foundation, the Volkswagen Foundation gives grants for research and the development of academic facilities.

Many other enterprises which in the United States are in the private sector are publicly owned and operated in West Germany. This applies to a large number of public utilities, to all communication systems from telephones to television and to transportation. Actually, then, the excellent record of economic development in Western Germany is the product of a mixed economy operating initially with a great deal of reconstruction assistance and then proceeding under a "bootstrap system" in which the public sector was deeply involved.

The overall effect of these incentives for private investment and a high degree of government intervention in support of prices and even of production levels in the mining industry was a very high share of investment in the gross national product. In the period 1950-59 investment in West Germany was 21.3 percent of the GNP as compared to 17 percent in the United States and 14.4 percent in the United Kingdom; from 1960 to 1964 the share of investment rose to 26.7 percent in West Germany while it dropped to 16.6 percent in the United States. In the United Kingdom the investment rate for that same period happens to be identical with that in this country.*

In the 1950's and in the early 1960's the annual growth rate in Western Europe and especially in West Germany was far in excess of the growth of the American economy. This gave rise at that time to a debate of why this should be so. The answer, however, should have been obvious. Western European countries had experienced a sharp drop in civilian output over a long period of time. During and immediately after the war consumer demand for new products and new housing had to be postponed. It took several years for consumer-goods production and residential construction to catch up with the accumulated purchasing power. Without large-scale new investment a new balance between consumer income and the supply of goods and services could not have been achieved. In the United States there had been a certain postponement of consumer demand during World War II, especially in the area of passenger cars and residential housing. However, the level of the civilian economy never dropped as low as it was

*From *Long Term Economic Growth 1860-1965,* U.S. Department of Commerce, Part IV, Table 10.

in Europe. It follows that once production systems were restarted and then expanded, growth rates especially in Western Germany would far exceed those in the United States. This was particularly true of the period after 1958, when there was a slowdown in the American economy which was not overcome until 1963.

It is unlikely that economic development in the 1970's will continue in West Germany at the hectic pace it held in the early 1960's. As we have seen, the high rates of growth had been made possible in the 1950's through the influx of German nationals who had been forced to leave Communist countries. The further expansion of activities could be handled only by the extensive use of foreign labor from southern Europe. Even with these additions to the labor force, factor transformation at an accelerated rate was necessary to keep up with rising activities. A calculation of the rate of growth consistent with full employment in West Germany predicated only on the natural increase of the labor force in that country and on further increases in productivity would yield far lower values than an equilibrium growth rate for the United States. In fact, it has been estimated that in the late 1960's the native German labor force would decline by a rate of 0.3 percent per annum. This is due to the high losses in World War II and the low birth rate in subsequent years. But the German economy will be increasingly burdened by the relatively high percentage of the population over 65 years which has been granted a very ample system of old-age benefits requiring joing employer-employee contributions of 15 percent of the gross earnings.

These social overhead costs will have to be met by an even greater emphasis on labor productivity. Factor transformation, an important aspect of economic development of Western Germany, will have to continue in the future in order to prevent a top-heavy economic structure and stagnation.

THE RAPID DEVELOPMENT OF THE JAPANESE ECONOMY

Up to about a hundred years ago the Empire of Japan, following as in so many other ways the example of China, had cut itself off from modern economic development as it had occurred in Western Europe with the onset of the seventeenth century. Unlike China, however, where centralized Imperial power was rather effective at least until the end of the eighteenth century and feudal territorial powers had been largely suppressed, a full feudal system with a weak central government headed by a shadow ruler, the Emperor, characterized the political and economic structure of Japan. As in China, the achievements of craftsmen and artists were high. There was, however, not even the beginning of industrialization prior to the contact with Commodore Perry in 1850. Somewhat earlier, in the Opium War (1839-42) the Chinese had been compelled by the British to open some of their ports to foreign trade. However, the Chinese reaction to this enforced contact with the technically far more advanced Western World was hostile. In Japan the encounter with the West led to an entirely different reaction. It culminated in the Meiji revolution of 1868.

Actually this was a revolution from the top down. It consisted in the assertion of a strong imperial power and the disestablishment of the feudal Shogunate which had run the country for centuries. In a way this emergence of centralized government over feudal systems and privileges is reminiscent of the strengthening of the monarchial power in European countries at the end of the Middle Ages. As in Europe it did not carry the connotation with it that the ruling-class structure based on a land accumulation system had disappeared completely. The great ability of the Japanese people of learning from other culture systems without losing their own national identity, which first had shown itself in the acceptance of many culture forms of the Chinese now was demonstrated also in the speed with which they succeeded to adapt themselves to modern industrial procedures. Within a few decades they were able to make a transition from a feudal-handicraft system to a modern industrial state.

This required also the adoption of a Western style political constitution. The constitution of the large German state of Prussia, which was dissolved by the Allied Powers after World War II, served as a model for Japan. This constitution dating back to 1851 introduced representative government without, however, impairing the executive power vested in the monarch. It was he who could appoint and dismiss the government, and while the Diet controlled the purse strings it could neither elect or discharge the cabinet appointed by the Sovereign. As in Prussia, the armed forces also enjoyed a special and somewhat privileged position within the state structure. This type of constitution was adopted in 1889 in Japan.

The immediate effect of the Meiji revolution was the formal abolishment of feudalism and the introduction of freedom of movement, of contract, and of entry into business. Simultaneously industrialization was pushed by the government. In fact, as had been the case under mercantilism in the seventeenth and eighteenth centuries in Europe with its subsidies to business corporations, the Japanese government assisted in the setting up of modern industrial activities. Railroad building started in 1870, and modern silk and cotton manufacturing enterprises were set up about the same time. There was a great emphasis on the development of mining, especially of copper and coal. In many cases the government itself was the initial operator of industrial enterprises, but toward the end of the nineteenth century most of them were transferred into the private sector. Very soon a tendency toward large-scale business concentration became noticeable. A business oligarchy the *zaibatsu* developed, headed by four huge combines which, however, remained under the family control of the owners.

In order to understand the unique pattern of economic development in Japan it is necessary to consider the fact that up to the 1950's the Japanese population experienced a very rapid rate of growth. The first population census taken in 1872 showed a total of 34.8 million people. A doubling of the population took place within fifty-seven years. In 1935 the population had reached 68.6 million. By 1957 it had grown to 90.7 million and in the 1960's it broke the 100-million mark.

At the onset of the Meiji revolution about one hundred years ago 80 percent of the Japanese population was living in agricultural households. With the development of industry and trade the share of the agricultural population declined steadily. By 1940 it had dropped to 41 percent. But unlike advanced Western countries, especially the United States, there was no drop in absolute numbers of the Japanese farm population. On the contrary, immediately after World War II the agricultural population rose substantially. Ten years after World War II agricultural employment was at about the same level that it had been prior to the outbreak of that conflict. Actually the average size of the family farm in Japan, always quite small, dropped even further in the postwar period. The land reform carried out at that time reduced land tenancy to less than 10 percent of the arable land, whereas before World War II, the vast majority of agricultural households still existed under tenancy arrangements or even as agricultural workers. Nevertheless agricultural output rose significantly after World War II, following the application of chemical fertilizer and of insecticides. The agricultural development of highly industralized Japan is an outstanding example of the feasibility of maintaining a fairly high percentage of agricultural employment while industry is being built up under conditions of factor transformation. The increase in farm output in Japan is due neither to merging of small farms into much larger units nor to mechanization. This has deminished the pressures on employment opportunities in the nonagricultural sector which are so typical of the development patterns in Latin America and even in the United States.

We have seen that in the first eighty years of the modern period of Japan the population rose at a very rapid pace. Even while Japan was under American military government some consideration has been given to the inauguration of measures designed to decelerate the population growth. Actually a most drastic method was adopted by the Japanese government which has been rejected almost everywhere else—legalized voluntary abortion. The effects of these legal changes were rather startling. The birth rate in Japan in the early 1960's dropped to the lowest level of any modern industrial country. Whereas in the period 1950-55 the annual growth of the Japanese labor force was still 3.7 percent reflecting the very high birth rate of the pre-World War II period, it had declined to 1.1 percent for the years 1960-64. By contrast the annual increase in the labor force in France rose from 0.2 percent in 1950-55 to 1.1 percent in the later period. In the United States the annual increase for the same years was 1.3 percent.

This extremely drastic change of the Japanese birth rate shows the willingness of the Japanese people to go along with policy objectives of the government. It can, therefore, be assumed that a reversal of the downward trend could also be brought about by this type of "social engineering." In fact in the late 1960's labor shortages began to develop in Japan. They were met initially by eliminating many types of low-wage employment especially of females, for instance, "escalator attendants" in department stores whose sole function had been to wipe the handrails of these installations.

While the agricultural population declined only relatively but not absolutely, Japan is an outstanding example of factor transformation in industry. As in England at the end of the eighteenth century, the Industrial Revolution in Japan had meant initially the building up of the textile industry. In 1930, 54.6 percent of the employment and 38 percent of the gross value of output originated with the Japanese textile industry.* By 1959 the production of machinery and vehicles had overtaken the textile industry. The share of employment in the metals industry rose from 5.5 percent in 1930 to 13.3 percent in 1959. Great increases also occurred in the chemical industry. This shift from light to heavy industries was facilitated by the retention of the high degree of concentration in large firms characteristic of the *zaibatsu* system. As in Germany, American occupation authorities initiated a policy of decartelization leading to the formal

*The information used in this section is taken primarily from the comprehensive Statistical Appendix attached to G. C. Allen, *Japan's Economic Expansion*, New York, Oxford University Press, 1965.

disestablishment of complex business combines controlled by a few families. But as in Germany these changes did not eliminate close cooperation among successor firms and their executive personnel nor did it lessen the close cooperation between the private sector and government agencies concerned with economic development.

The build-up of heavy industries together with the growth of agricultural output and of domestic and international trade led to extremely high values of annual increases in the Japanese gross national product. While there were significant short-run decreases—for instance, from 7.9 percent in 1957 to 3.2 percent in 1958—there were also "great leaps forward" in recent years such as those of 14 percent in 1961 and 12 percent in 1963. All these changes are measured in constant money units. The high degree of factor transformation is also indicated by the ratios of investment in producers equipment. While in 1951 this ratio was 11.2 percent of the gross national expenditure, it rose to 22.9 percent in 1961. Inevitably this is reflected in the rapid rise of industrial production in Japan. The output of capital goods on the basis of 1960 equal to 100.0 rose to 153.9 in 1963. Nondurable consumer goods rose by 30.8 percent in the same period. Energy production of utilities rose by 38.0 percent during the same span of time.

A particularly sharp increase occurred in shipbuilding. While in 1953 ships with a gross tonnage of 557,000 were built, the output had risen to 2.4 million tons in 1963. In the same period steel ingot production rose from 7.7 million to 31.5 million tons. In this short ten-year period Japan had been able to build up its steel industry to the point where it was contesting West Germany for third place among the industrial nations of the world.

The high rate of capital investment has brought about steep increases in labor productivity. In this way it was possible for Japanese industry to increase output much faster than employment in industry. Such a condition is typical of economic development through factor transformation. Increases in physical productivity measured in output per worker were consistently higher in Japan than in the United States, the Soviet Union, or West Germany. It was 9.1 percent in 1959 and over 8 percent in the two following years. While the Chinese Communists in the 1950's tried to stage a Great Leap Forward and failed, the Japanese in the 1960's without proclaiming such ambitious targets actually went into a phase of accelerated economic development unsurpassed in any peacetime economy.

As a result of this high rate of growth the value of exports from Japan increased very rapidly from over $4 billion in 1960 to $5.5 billion in 1963.

At the same time a significant change took place in the composition of Japanese exports reflecting the investment in the heavy and producer goods industries. Whereas prior to World War II textiles accounted for more than 50 percent of the exports from Japan, their share had declined to 22.8 percent in 1963. On the other hand, exports of metals and metal products had risen to 17.3 percent and that of machinery and vehicles to 27.1 percent of all exports.

Because of the limitations in arable land and the lack of fuels, especially oil, Japan is constantly in need of imports. However, there is an indication that the excess of imports over exports in Japan is declining. Prior to World War II food imports accounted for a far larger share in total imports than in the 1960's. This is the result of the increase of farm output, which as we have seen was carried out without a displacement of the agricultural population. However, there has been a substantial increase in the import of oil and coal due to the rising requirements of industry. For this reason Japan has built up export and shipbuilding industries at an unprecedented rate. Wage differentials operate in favor of Japan and competition is heavily felt in the United States and elsewhere.

FURTHER OBSERVATIONS ON GERMANY AND JAPAN

The great success of West Germany and Japan in recovering from the economic (as distinct from the political) effects of World War II and in making great strides thereafter in accelerated development raises the question to what extent these two cases can serve as a model. While both countries show that high levels of elementary school education, achievement-oriented workers and employees and efficient management are indispensable requirements for a successful drive toward higher level of production, it is necessary to stress some of the unique factors that facilitated the favorable course of events in these two countries. A consideration of these circumstances will protect us from generalizing on German and Japanese development without due qualifications.

Although in both countries factor transformation played an increasing role in achieving high rates of development, both countries benefited in an originally unexpected way from a vast influx of nationals which had to leave areas falling under foreign control. While many German nationals moved into West Germany, augmenting the labor force substantially, a considerable number of Japanese who had been settled in Korea had to return to their home country. Both countries also were helped by early postwar policies forcing them into complete disarmament. In a period of the incipient cold war in which the victorious countries had to allocate vast resources of labor and of capital to the maintenance and the continuous improvement of a military posture, such a diversion of factors from reconstruction and economic development did not take place in the first years after the end of World War II in West Germany and Japan. Both countries were able to avoid unmanageable inflation as economic development accelerated. Factor transformation enabled them to keep prices of exports on a level that did not impair their competitive position on world markets. For this reason both countries experienced a rapid growth of the volume and value of their exports.

It seems evident that economic development can occur under a variety of institutional structures. Germany and Japan have retained the principle of private ownership on means of production, although they permitted a high degree of concentration. And whereas in the Soviet Union public ownership of industry was continued, in the 1960's the consumer industries were given greater flexibility and permitted to establish direct lines of communication with state-owned retail outlets. In the Soviet Union great stress is being placed on increasing labor productivity which is lagging far behind the standards in the United States and Western Europe. The Soviet system, like Germany and Japan, places great stress on factor transformation as the method of choice in economic development.

We have seen, however, that this is only one of the possible roads toward economic development. The record established by Japan and Germany do not of themselves justify the conclusion that they could be applied everywhere regardless of the conditions of the "human capital" of managerial skill and labor efficiency. It is in this area that the influence of the history of economic systems must be considered in order to select realistic methods for economic development.

In Japan a continuity of government and a basic integrity of the territory was maintained after the military surrendered. On the other hand, West Germany experienced a suspension of native national government for a period of four years. Furthermore, West Germany represents only about two-thirds of the total territory of Germany as it was left after World War II. Both countries, however, have in common the fact that drastic political changes were not accompanied by profound structural transformations of the economy. In fact, the economic substructure proved to be more continuous and resilient than the political superstructure. In a way, the economic development of Japan and of West Germany shows the irrelevance of much of nineteenth century political and economic ideology if applied in the latter part of the twentieth century.

chapter 7

Development Beyond Affluence: The American Case

At the very beginning of this volume it was stressed that economic development is open-ended. As an economy goes through various stages, from early development according to the sectoral growth pattern to accelerated development under the impact of factor transformation, new tangible targets are coming into view continuously in terms of an increase in productive capacity, diversification of output, a general improvement in material standards of living, and the building up of social overhead capital including educational and cultural institutions. Since all these things are tangible and physical and—quite apart from their value aspects—are also quantitative and measurable, the conclusion might be drawn that once all these material advances have been realized there would be no need for further growth. An advanced system could then settle down on a high level of capacity, earmarking each year a considerable proportion of the gross national product for maintenance, renewal, and replacement of the great array of assets already accumulated. In this imaginary state social energies could be shifted from a concern with further growth and expansion to a growing involvment with the improvement of quality of material and cultural aspects of society.

However, such an end phase of economic development—or, as it were, a posteconomic stage of human history—is not in sight. This is obvious for the greater part of mankind which in the last decades of the twentieth century is struggling to maintain or to even achieve a precarious balance between an increasing population, food production, and basic educational and residential facilities. However, it is also true for highly advanced industrialized countries. They are under continuous pressures to advance further on the path of economic development. They cannot slow down or settle down without facing serious dangers of economic and social deterioration and disintegration. In this chapter we will investigate these problems of development of an already highly advanced system as they arise in the United States. By implication, such analysis also will have relevance to other highly developed countries, especially in Northwestern Europe. In Chapter 3 a summary outline of the problems arising at very advanced levels of economic development have already been outlined in Scenario 5. We will now proceed to a more detailed analysis of this situation.

PRESSURES FOR CONTINUED DEVELOPMENT

The main reasons why economic development must continue in advanced countries—especially in the United States—regardless of already achieved high levels of living, are the continuously increasing demand for employment and the rapid transformation of factors. These two trends are actually at odds with each other. On the one hand the annual addition to the labor force requires an annual rise of employment opportunities large enough to accomodate the new workers and to prevent the accumulation of high rates of unemployment among the youngest segments of the labor force. On the other hand, the ever-increasing use of advanced equipment in production, office operations, and data processing seems to reduce unit labor requirements within the system as a whole. Now we will show in the next section how these conflicting trends were reconciled in the United States after World War II. As a first step it is necessary to analyze in some greater detail the operation of these two factors which force the American economy to maintain a high rate of forward momentum even in a peace-time setting if serious dislocations are to be avoided.

In the decade 1960-70 the population of the United States increased by 1.8 percent per annum while the labor force rose at a higher rate, 2.2 percent per year. Due to a significant drop in the birth rate it is projected that for the period 1970-80 the population will grow only by 1.6 percent per annum. However, the labor force will rise yearly by 1.8 percent.* While in percentages there will be a decline in the annual increase of the labor force in the 1970's in actual numbers due to the overall growth of the population, about the same number of jobs—15 million—will have to be added during that decade as were being created during the 1960's. We will see later in this chapter that the ever-improving employment record was closely associated with the stepping-up of national defense expenditures during that period. In the 1970's the ability of the American economy to

*Manpower Report of the President, 1967, Table E-7.

add 1.5 million additional employment opportunities each year may be predicated not on the dynamics of war but on the ability to generate peacetime substitutes for full-employment levels closely connected with the high rate of government spending for national defense. But while the total number of employment opportunities required each year will remain high, the proportion of the population in the labor force (the labor-force participation rate) is expected to continue its steady advance. In 1965 it was 56.4 percent of the population age 14 and over: in 1980 it is expected to rise to 58.2 percent. Virtually all of this increase will be due to the still growing share of women in the American labor force. It is expected to grow from 36.5 percent in 1965 to 40 percent in 1980.

At first sight an increase in labor-force participation in a society already characterized by a high degree of development and affluence seems to be paradoxical. The contradiction becomes more pronounced if we allow for the fact that in this prosperous system in the 1960's at least 15 percent of the people were still living in a state of poverty. But the latter group consists largely of people outside the labor force. We can also reverse the statement and say that a considerable proportion of the poor are in that condition because they are not or can no longer be members of the labor force. The increase of labor-force participation in the United States emanates, therefore, from the prosperity, not from the poverty sector of the economy. The need for employment outside the house evidenced by still rising female labor-force participation rates is brought forth by the very structure of economic progress occurring in an advanced system. One aspect of rising affluence is the ever-declining share of such necessary expenditures as food and clothing in the budget of middle- and high-income families. Discretionary spending can assume vastly greater proportions. It is directed toward automobiles, durable household goods, travel, and last but not least education. This type of demand requires an ever-rising income of the family as a spending unit. The transformation of the labor force into a predominantly white-collar group with steadily rising educational requirements causes pressures on family budgets which very often are relieved only by the reentry of the housewife into the labor force. In other words, the great improvements in levels of living and of education, far from reducing the labor force, are in fact developing a dynamism that in turn produces a steadily increasing aggregate demand for employment.

We now turn our attention to a simultaneous trend moving in the opposite direction: the sharp decline in unit labor requirements in large segments of American industry. This trend is clearly evident in the annual

increases in output per manpower that have occurred in the first part of
the 1960's. In the mining industry the productivity of labor increased at
an annual rate of 4.2 percent. In fact, this increase was so great that even
after allowances made for annual increases in compensations per hour the
unit labor costs in mining declined by 0.7 percent per year between 1959
and 1966.* In transportation, unit labor costs declined in the same period
by 0.8 percent per annum. The greatest decrease per year in unit labor
costs occurred in communications, where it reached 1 percent. Decreases
were also noted in public utilities. In manufacturing industries output rose
annually by 5.8 percent between 1959 and 1966, output per man-hour 3.6
percent, and compensation 3.8 percent. As a result only 0.3 percent increases per year occurred in unit labor cost in manufacturing. However,
this slight annual increase in unit labor cost must be seen in the context of
vast structural changes in employment in the manufacturing industry that
are characteristic of the new type of factor transformation taking place in
a highly advanced system, most notably in the United States. Factor transformation leading to accelerated growth and a decline in unit labor requirements continues to be very strong so far as the employment of production or blue-collar workers is concerned. This is clearly shown by a
comparison between changes in employment and increases in production
in the manufacturing industry. Between 1957 and 1967 employment in
manufacturing increased from 17.2 to 19.3 million. The index of production in manufacturing on a basis of 1957-59 = 100 rose from 100.7 percent in 1957 to 157.8 percent in 1967. While total employment in
manufacturing in the same period increased about 12 percent the output
of the industry rose far in excess of 50 percent in a ten-year period. In fact
while unit labor costs rose by 0.3 percent per annum, output rose by 4.7
percent yearly in the period 1957-67. However, this overall picture does
not tell the whole story. The employees in the manufacturing industry are
subdivided into production and nonproduction workers. The number of
production workers in 1957 was 13.2 million and rose by only 1 million to
14.2 million in 1967. That is, while overall employment in manufacturing
increased by 12 percent employment of production workers increased on
7 percent. The unit-labor-cost increase in manufacturing is, therefore, due
only to the ever-rising ratio of nonproduction workers in these industries.
Whereas in 1957 23.2 percent of the employees in manufacturing were
nonproduction workers their share in 1967 was about 26 percent.

Here we encounter another aspect of factor transformation. As the

*Economic Report of the President, February 1968, Table 18.

significance of research and of scientific methods of management increases a change in the composition of the labor force is taking place. Factor transformation does no longer affect only the capital-labor ratio, it increasingly also extends to the proportion between manual and clerical workers with the share of the former declining. Actually in the United States a white-collar economy emerged in the 1950's.

This has vast significance for the analysis of further growth of highly advanced countries which are compelled to continue economic development beyond the levels of conventional affluence in order to maintain full employment of a growing labor force. Before we address ourselves in greater detail to this problem in the next section it is well to reiterate that the pressures for continuous expansion persist regardless of the very high plateaus of production, employment, and income already achieved. Up to the latter part of the 1960's, the steady decline in the labor requirements of production workers was more than offset by the steady rise in the demand for white-collar workers. As an advanced economy reaches the stage at which further growth is deemed necessary to maintain full employment rather than to deal with scarcities, the conceptualization of equilibrium growth rates requires reexamination.

GROWTH RATES AT VARIOUS STAGES
OF DEVELOPMENT

Growth rates vary according to the phase of economic development. An economic system making a transition to industrialization will show very high growth rates for the simple statistical reason that even a slight initial progression beyond a zero level will loom very large. In the United States the annual growth rate of the gross national product was 4.5 percent in the period from 1870 to 1913.* This was far in excess of growth rates of other countries in the process of industrialization during that period. The corresponding rates for Germany were 2.8 percent, for the United Kingdom 2.1 percent and for Japan 3.3 percent. With this great build-up in industrial capacity prior to World War I, a considerable slowdown occurred in the United States even during that conflict and in the ensuing prosperity period ending in 1929. Between 1913 and 1929 the annual growth rate of the American economy dropped to 2.8 percent. It continued high in Japan but declined to less than 1 percent in Germany

*Long-Term Economic Growth, 1860-1965, U.S. Department of Commerce, Table VII, Part IV.

and in the United Kingdom. From 1929 to 1933 the GNP in current dollars in the United States collapsed from $103.1 billion to $55.6 billion. Even in 1939 the GNP had not reached again the level of ten years earlier.

After World War II the growth rate in the United States rose high above the interwar level. For the period 1950 to 1964 it averaged 3.6 percent per annum. This, however, was considerably below the rates achieved in Japan (9.9 percent), Germany (7 percent), and France (4.8 percent). The reason for the much higher rates in Germany are obvious; massive wartime destruction caused a vastly reduced productive capacity and extreme housing shortage to prevail after World War II. As a result annual growth rates were very high, reverting to the pattern of early development situations referred to at the beginning of this section. Furthermore, as we have seen in the preceding chapter, Japan and Germany stressed factor transformation with great intensity especially in the latter part of the 1950-64 period. In France the high rate of growth was due to a deliberate decision taken after World War II under the Monnet Plan to increase the heavy industry and energy sector of the economy through a succession of four-year plans in which growth patterns were agreed upon between government, management, and labor and enacted by Parliament.

While the growth rates in the United States as well as in the other countries mentioned here can be explained largely up to the early 1960's in terms of a balanced-growth model in which an expansion of productive capacity in heavy and light industries and in social overhead cost played a decisive role, after that period new basic factors became operative especially in the United States. They deserve close attention because on the proper interpretation of this most recent type of development depends our comprehension and our ability to formulate policies of growth beyond affluence.

For the first time since before World War I annual growth rates in the United States began to rise above the 4 percent level. In fact for the whole period 1960 to 1965 when they averaged out a 4.7 percent they were slightly higher than at the turn of the century when immigration—and therefore increases in the labor force—reached high numerical values. Acutally this 4.7 percent figure for the period 1960-65 does not tell the whole story because the year 1961 was considered a depression year. After 1965 annual rates of growth of the economy exceeded 5 percent in constant dollars and reached more than 8 percent in dollars of each year. It is of utmost urgency for the economic analyst and especially the theoretician of economic development to study with great care and without conceptual bias the structure of this newest trend of an advanced system.

The need to approach this complex situation with a fresh mind is clearly borne out by the frequent but misleading application of obsolete business-cycle concepts to the continuous upswing of the American economy from 1961 to 1968. It has been asserted by professional economists in and out of government that this period represented the longest "recovery" from a recession ever recorded in American economic history. Very often this type of analysis is connected with the assertion that modern economics with its arsenal of tools of fiscal and monetary policies has solved the age-old problem of economic instability. It is said that the instruments now available to government and to business are so finely tuned that economic development can be "managed"—accelerated or decelerated to fit into overall goals such as maintenance of employment and price stability.

It is not the purpose of our present analysis to contradict the prevailing optimism with regard to the effectiveness of fiscal and monetary policies. However, it must be pointed out that in the United States time lags have opened up in the enactment of tax changes required by such fiscal policies. Such time lags in themselves form no objection to the theory of a fiscal approach to stabilizing economic development. However, this is an area in which we appreciate the meaning of the old-fashioned term "Political Economy," which seems to point out that decision models in economics somehow must be made operative in a constitutional setting which may not automatically yield to the postulates of purely economic analysis. More important is the fact that the interpretation of the unprecedented period of economic "upswing" in the United States as the longest period of recovery is concealing two important factors that must be considered realistically. The first factor is of a long-run nature, and therefore of great significance for development theory: it is a transformation of the labor force itself into a predominantly nonproduction group and the changing structure and parameters of the demand for labor itself as it occurs in the phase of development beyond affluence.

The second factor operative in the American economy in the 1960's, especially after 1965 was a stepping-up of national defense expenditures and employment as a result of the Vietnam war. Due to this "one-shot" development the question remains open how economic development of an advanced white-collar economy can be sustained indefinitely. The full employment brought about by the second factor is a random event which cannot be fitted either into conventional business cycle analysis or into the equally conventional fiscal plus monetary approach to economic analysis and policy.

The actual growth rates of the economy of the United States after 1965 do not only exceed any progression experienced in the United States apart from the rise from the depression lows of 1939 to the heights of war production in 1945, they also exceed the equilibrium growth rates for a steady advance of the system required by the dynamic model of Harrod.* According to Harrod the natural growth rate of an economic system is determined by two variables: the annual increase in the labor force and the annual increase in the productivity of labor. It should be noted that these two factors can be measured quantitatively without much difficulty. Census data permit the projection of the annual growth of the labor force for a period of at least fifteen years. Labor productivity can be measured in various ways—for instance output per worker or output per man hour. It is also possible to compare the revenues of a firm or industry with the total employment cost incurred in producing these earnings. The output per man-hour is more frequently used to represent changes in productivity than the other yardstick mentioned here. Obviously as one or both variables show greater positive changes, the Harrod type macroeconomic growth rate is bound to increase also. In the 1950's there prevailed agreement among most professional economists that a 3.4 percent per annum increase in the real GNP would satisfy the requirements of continued equilibrium growth. With a steep annual increase in the number of new workers during the 1960's and the spread of advanced technology boosting labor productivity, these growth rates were estimated to necessitate at least a 4.2 percent increase in the GNP. Actually the growth rate of the United States economy was less than this even in 1961. Then a steep rise ensued. As we have seen above the average growth rate of the American economy in the period of 1960-65 was 4.7 percent per annum. This was higher than the necessary rate according to the dynamic model of Harrod. But it took this actual, higher rate, to reduce unemployment from 6.7 percent in 1961 to 3.8 percent in 1967.

This experience with the relation between growth rates and levels of employment in the highly advanced American economy was an indication that up from a certain point the natural growth rates as generally understood in macrodynamic growth models are no longer sufficient to maintain such a system in dynamic equilibrium that is to say to accommodate into the labor force each year the new workers and to maintain full employment even while a production worker productivity is rising steeply. Actually under such conditions the growth rate itself must be growing each year in order to

*See the extended presentation and analysis of this problem in William J. Baumol, *Economic Dynamics*, 2d ed., New York, Macmillan 1959.

prevent accumulation of unemployment among the youngest age groups within the labor force and actual labor displacement as mechanization and automation are spreading throughout the system.

Now it is a fact that the American economy in the 1960's has actually performed according to this postulate of accelerated growth. Every year after 1964 the increase of the GNP was at a higher rate than the preceeding year. Early in 1968 a yearly growth rate of 10 percent was indicated at least in current dollars. This led to the enactment of monetary policies, increases in individual and corporate income taxes and in prime interest rates. As a result of this unprecedented advance of the American economy unemployment declined further from 4.5 percent in 1965 to 3.8 percent in 1967. Actually these levels of unemployment would have been considered completely unobtainable in the 1930's. Even at a later period it was commonly believed that a satisfactory level of full employment would be indicated when actual unemployment had dropped to 5 percent of the labor force. This viewpoint is no longer acceptable. In the highly advanced economy of the United States there has been a simultaneous development of acute labor shortages—for instance, in the whole field of medicine—and a high level of persistent unemployment among the less skilled and less educated.

It cannot be the purpose of an employment policy operating within a strict economic frame of reference to reduce unemployment to zero. Labor economists have never equated full employment with 100 percent employment. In fact such a tightness on the labor market would be just as undesirable as would be a situation in which all residential dwellings had a 100 percent occupancy rate. It seems then that employment of the unemployables is a problem which must be worked out in a social and political rather than in a strictly economic context. No further increase in the annual rate of aggregate spending is likely to reduce this type of unemployment any further. On the other hand, any slowdown in the rate of growth would push unemployment to higher levels. Even a slight decline from a previous year would considerably aggravate the situation on the labor market and threaten to disrupt social stability.

The conclusion cannot be avoided that there is a close relation between levels of economic development and rates of growth required to maintain an advanced system in balance. As systems reach a condition of general affluence—which does not, as experience shows, preclude pockets of poverty—growth rates must continue to rise. We again come to a point where it can be seen clearly that economic development is open-ended.

Now it might appear that the American economy which experienced (as it too often is said) the longest period of uninterrupted economic growth in the 1960's has in fact reached a stage in which further development becomes self-sustaining and which every advance in national income and employment exercises a feedback effect which pushes the system to ever-higher levels of performance. The image that presents itself seems to indicate that the general pattern of economic development from early stages of sectoral growth, to later stages of factor transformation would eventually lead to continuous, self-generating further expansion. As Baumol has pointed out, this is implied in the mathematics of the Harrod model of economic dynamics. But to conclude that what is mathematically indicated will actually occur in the real world of an economic system would be a dangerous logical shortcut. We will now demonstrate that the experience of the American economy in recent times does not justify the assumption that the problem of self-sustaining growth which posits itself in an advanced system has been solved. The question whether it is possible for a system to maintain development after it has reached the stage of affluence is still open. In the next section we will examine the actual performance of the American economy by taking into account the fact that national defense spending has assumed a major role in the total structure. The question remains unanswered whether the momentum of a defense-oriented economy of a technological society can be maintained if there is a change of the direction of the spending stream from the military to the civilian areas of society.

NATIONAL DEFENSE AND ECONOMIC GROWTH

The impact of huge expenditures for national defense varies with different stages of economic development. In the Soviet Union communism committed itself to rapid industrialization of a vast country which up to that time had not gone beyond the stage of infant industries. This brought about very large statistical growth rates in the 1930's, although the actual increase in physical volume of output makes it somewhat doubtful whether this growth could be fitted into the concept of maximum-speed development.

Advances in technology have revolutionized warfare and weapons technology perhaps at an even greater rate than they have changed production systems and procedures in the private sector. Hence an effective national defense requires a substantial investment in heavy industries and a high level of knowledge and skill in engineering and design of modern equipment. Furthermore, continuous improvements in weapons and delivery systems, especially if speeded up by the competition between superpowers, creates a high degree of obsolescence, making necessary continuous renewal and redesigning of all defense items.

In the Soviet Union which went prior to World War II through a phase of early development, the superimposition of a vast defense sector on the projects for industrial development contributed in large measure to the "unbalanced growth" which characterized this phase of the evolution of the Soviet Communist system. Only in the late 1960's did efforts become really effective to correct this built-in imbalance by placing greater efforts into the improvements and diversification of consumer goods output in the USSR.

When Keynesian policies were first applied in the 1930's in the Western world, stressing the role of government in maintaining and if need be supplementing aggregate spending, national defense expenditures—especially in the United States—were a very insignificant item of government spending. In 1929 federal expenditures were amounting to $1.3 billion or 1 percent of the gross national product. In 1939 total federal expenditures had risen to $5.1 billion, whereas the GNP had dropped as compared to 1929 to $90.5 billion. Total federal spending had, therefore, risen from 1 percent of GNP to about 5 percent. However, national defense spending which had been stepped up during the 1930's amounted to only one fourth of federal spending. The greatest part of federal expenditures were directed toward the financing of work relief projects. It should be noted that the drastic increase of total federal expenditures, actually a rise of 400 percent in a ten-year period, apparently was not able to lift the American economy out of the depression and to reduce unemployment substantially. In fact, in 1939 unemployment still was 17.2 percent of the labor force. While there had been a substantial improvement over the absolute low of the Great Depression in 1932, the best that can be said of this decade of American economic history is that it represents a period of stagnation or zero economic development.

Since then there has been a steady development of the American economy, interrupted only infrequently and for a short period of time by recessions which must be termed mild as compared to the experiences of the nineteenth century and especially the 1930's. Such recessions occurred in 1949, 1954, and 1958. Between 1958 and 1961 there was a period of less than equilibrium growth, resulting as we have seen before in rates of unemployment close to 7 percent of the labor force in 1958 and in 1961. By and large, however, since 1940 there has been a high rate of economic development. As we have seen earlier in this chapter, in the middle 1960's the annual growth rate of the American economy achieved an all-time high exceeding even the steep annual progressions of the turn of the century.

No doubt a part of this growth is related to the variables contained in the Harrod models. The labor force of the United States increased from 56 million in 1940 to over 80 million in 1967. Labor productivity was increasing at a slow rate in the 1940's. In the latter period the productivity of production workers rose more rapidly. However, toward the end of the period under discussion here these improvements were offset to a certain extent by the ever increasing share of nonproduction workers in total employment costs. It would be a futile enterprise to speculate what would have happened to the American economy if it had not entered in 1940 a new era in which defense spending began to play a very large role in total public spending. The fact is that aggregate spending by government which in the 1930's had focused on work relief and similar expenditures now shifted to procurement for national defense and the maintenance of a vast military establishment. The government became the largest single customer of industry, advancing funds even during World War II for the expansion of production capacity in the steel and automobile industry, and after the war encouraging further growth of industrial investment in expectation of a continued high level of defense spending through favorable write-off provisions in tax laws.

While all these changes took place the institutional structure of the United States remained the same. It is, therefore, possible to describe the American economy as a private free-enterprise system in the 1960's just as it had existed in the 1920's. However, this does not answer the question whether a limitation of government expenditures for national defense to the scope it had in the earlier period would have resulted in the type of economic development which actually did take place. It is sometimes argued that it makes no difference what the mix of aggregate expenditures is, especially what proportion of the total spending originates in the private and what part comes from the public sector. Some economists feel that it is the total amount of spending rather than its composition that determines levels of employment and rates of economic development. This argument does have validity only in a system with limited production possibilities. Only under such conditions can it be assumed that a reduction in public spending will almost automatically be replaced by an increase in private spending. The argument would also be applicable to imbalanced types of economic development in which as we have seen consumer demand is deliberately being repressed over considerable periods of time. This was actually the case in the United States during World War II when private consumption expenditures between 1940 and 1945 rose only by about $30 billion in 1958 prices whereas the GNP rose by almost $130 billion in the same period of time.

A comparison between large scale spending for relief in the 1930's and government spending for national defense in the 1950's and 1960's shows, however, that there are vast differences in the economic effects between these two types of spending. At the height of World War II national defense spending rose to more than 40 percent of the GNP. By 1967 it was 10 percent of the GNP as compared to 1 percent in the 1920's. To engage in analyses of long upswings of the American economy and to indulge in conjectures about self-sustaining patterns of economic development in the United States without reference to the structural changes in public spending from relief to defense represents a type of theoretical thinking that would not meet the test of relevance. It is obvious that the very nature of technological progress require increasingly sophisticated delivery systems for complicated weapons and equally complex advanced design aircraft and corresponding defense installations. Countless other items of military hardware generate a demand for the products of the electronics, aircraft, automobile, and other industries, which while making necessary continuous expansion of production facilities nevertheless generates a never fully satisfied demand for scientific, professional, and otherwise highly skilled workers commanding high earnings. Unlike the subsistence wages paid out to workers on public work projects, the earnings of skilled personnel in the employment of private industry engaged in defense production are a substantial addition to the income stream and are bound to have a high multiplier effect. In any economy with a strong defense sector but without restrictions on consumer or business spending, the injection of defense spending of the scope and character it has in the United States is bound to generate high rates of economic growth year after year. If we just look at the GNP series it may appear that the problem of development beyond affluence has been solved. Unemployment in 1968 was below 4 percent of the labor force as compared to close to 7 percent in 1961. Despite steeper annual increases in prices, the per capita income in 1958 dollars was more than $400 a year higher in 1967 than in 1961. In the same period personal consumption expenditures had risen by more than $100 million.

An academic approach to the problem of further development of highly advanced systems cannot content itself with this type of description. It is necessary to ask more specifically what factors were operative in bringing about this accelerated development. Only if such questions are asked and answered will it be possible to make informed judgments on the likely course of sustained growth in the future. This probing will have to take into account one short-run development: the stepping up of the Vietnam was effort in 1965 and two longer-run structural changes in the American economy. We will have to consider the change in the composition of employment with its effects on employment costs, realized income of wage and salary workers and labor productivity. Furthermore, we have to come to grips with the fact that even accelerated development has not lessened the incidence of unemployment in marginal groups of the labor market. Far from relieving pressures on state and local finance, the period of accelerated growth has actually increased them.

We have seen that in the last quarter-century public spending for purposes other than relief has gone up considerably, thereby strengthening the total demand for workers as it emanates from the private and the public sectors. While a great deal of this demand originates on the state and local levels, the federal government through its large-scale spending for national defense has generated a substantial amount of employment in the "private" sector of the economy. Prior to the stepping up of the Vietman war there had actually been a slight decline in employment in private industry directly attributable to federal spending. Employment related to federal purchases of goods and services from private industry was 3.7 million in 1962. It was 3.3 million in 1965.* In actual numbers this amounted to an employment of 1,390,200 wage and salary earners in manufacturing in the fiscal year 1965 or 7.9 percent of total employment in this section of the economy. In the fiscal year 1967 defense-related employment in manufacturing had risen by 737,700. Now 10.5 percent of total manufacturing employment was directly generated by defense spending. In the service industries defense-related employment rose from 2 percent in fiscal 1965 to 2.5 percent in 1967.[†]

Total employment rose by about 3.3 million between 1965 and 1967. Now it is significant that almost 1 million of this additional employment can be accounted for by stepped-up defense expenditures of the federal government with the private sector. Another 1.4 million increase in employment during that period was caused directly by state and local governments. In 1965 state and local governments employed 7.5 million people; in 1967 total employment with these branches of government had risen to 8.9 million. It is clear then that the sectors of the economy generating the

*Manpower Report of the President, April 1967, Table 6.

[†] Richard P. Oliver, "The Employment Effect of Defense Expenditures," Monthly Labor Review, September 1967.

greatest additional demand for employment were in defense-related industries and in state and local government. It follows that the accelerated growth pattern of the American economy which alone accounts for the reduction of unemployment to less than 4 percent in the 1960's does not supply evidence that self-sustaining growth of the American economy can be brought about by the expansion of the private sector alone.

It is an easy analytical proposition to set up a model of the American economy 1965-75 under the assumption that the stepping up of the Vietnam war would not have occurred in 1965.*

If the growth patterns 1961-64 rather than the actual higher ones prevailed after 1965 had continued, substantial unemployment would have remained. In the absence of very determined efforts to counteract the trend toward less than equilibrium growth of the American economy, unemployment would have tended to rise year after year. According to these estimates the unemployment rate for 1975 would be about 12.2 percent of the labor force. This still would be significantly below that of 1937, the "best year" of the Great Depression, when unemployment dropped to 14.3 percent of the labor force. Just because this tendency toward unemployment still would leave the American labor market as a whole in a far better condition than it was in the 1930's, this projection of possible unemployment in the 1970's is entirely plausible. However, in sharp contrast to the economic crisis of the 1930's unemployment in the 1970's even approaching the estimate given here would aggravate the social crisis dangerously in the United States. To prevent such a possibility from turning into an actuality, vast efforts must be taken. But in order to do so it is necessary to become fully aware of the role that government spending for the products of industry and the vast increase in direct employment by government has played in reducing unemployment during the 1960's in generating a rate of growth far exceeding the requirements of the dynamic model of Harrod.

In the preceding paragraph we have dealt with a short-run situation which must be properly recognized in order to stop us from making straight-line projections of development beyond affluence for the 1970's based on the exceptional circumstances of the mid-1960's. There are, however, longer-run structural changes in operation which also must be considered in coming to grips with the problems posited by the need to sustain growth in a system which is already highly advanced.

One aspect of this progress is the great elaboration of wage structure and the improvement of social security systems. The latter have led to a

*Full Employment in 1975," Senior Research Project No. 10, Fordham University, 1967.

very steep increase in transfer payments in the receipts and expenditures of the federal sector of the national income accounts. In fact, in the decade from 1959 to 1969 transfer payments during the fiscal year rose from $21.6 billion to $49.9 billion.* Fringe benefits in collective agreements and other work arrangements provide for additional huge transfers into company pension funds. These funds have grown very rapidly and by the end of the 1960's they were about to break through the $100-billion ceiling. They have become the most powerful concentration of capital and investment funds in the private sector. Social security benefits and contributions to old-age insurance are slated for continuous increases through the 1970's. For this reason transfer payments are bound to increase in the future as they have in the 1960's. Higher payroll taxes for social insurance and transfers of funds to company pension systems add to the total employment costs. The difference between these costs, which include employers contributions to social insurance and deposits with private company funds and gross earnings of wage and salary workers, became greater at an accelerated rate in the 1960's.

Prior to the great changes in wage structures of the 1930's the difference between employees' total compensation and their wages and salaries was minimal. In 1960 total compensation of employees amounted to $294.2 billion and wages and salaries paid out were $270.8 billion. Seven years later in 1967 total compensation had risen to $469.6 billion, whereas wages and salaries amounted to $423.7 million. That is, the difference between total employment cost and gross earnings of labor continued to widen in the 1960's. These developments have great significance for the problem of sustaining growth beyond affluence. Every increase in total compensation of employees due to a rise in employers contributions to social security or to welfare funds is accounted for in the total national income. These "payments before wages" are factor costs of labor which are not related to current production or to consumption. They build-up "deferred incomes" paid out when wage and salary workers have retired. Every time these payments before wages rise, the GNP goes up. It follows that the increase in the national income has risen faster than employment itself in recent years.

At this advanced phase of economic development the need to establish optimum goals of employment reappears. In order to prevent a dangerous spread of pockets of poverty in a generally affluent society, employment cost of such marginal workers cannot be viewed within a purely private microeconomic context. Efforts to reduce the poverty sector of an

*Economic Report of the President, February 1968, Table B62.

affluent society to an absolute minimum must be made. The National Advisory Commission of Civil Disorders* has proposed a five-year plan for the construction of 6 million low- and moderate-cost housing units. Such a rate of building construction is entirely feasible in the United States, especially if compared with the speed of reconstruction of residential housing in certain European countries after World War II. But in order for this vast scheme to be really effective, there must be a great improvement in city planning and an agreement with organized labor in the construction trades to permit large-scale employment of residents of the areas to be rebuilt who at present are at the edges of or actually outside the labor market. Only in this manner can goals of maximum employment be reached in an affluent society. Actually demand for white-collar workers ranging from systems analysts to clerical employees has begun to rise steeply. This is an indication that strictly marginal-cost considerations are no longer entertained by those employers who can afford to operate at optimum rather than at maximum rates of return on their investment. The same approach might become necessary in construction projects of the type outlined here. Nevertheless profits of American corporations after taxes has risen substantially in a short period of time from $32.2 billion in 1962 to $47.2 billion in 1967.

The experience of growth and development of the American economy demonstrates very clearly that in the last twenty-five years public spending for the products of industry and for a vastly increased volume of employment by state and local governments has accounted largely for the maintenance of full employment and for growth rates required by a system characterized by high annual increases in the labor force and in labor productivity. It would be unrealistic to expect that at any foreseeable time in the future the whole burden of maintaining the necessary forward momentum of the American economy could be shifted to the private sector. Nevertheless there are certain clearly discernible long-run developments which may point to certain self-corrections of the economic structure quite independent from government participation and spending which may lessen somewhat the pressures of the variables contained in Harrod's macrodynamic model.

In his short volume *The Stages of Economic Growth,* W. W. Rostow[†] thought that he had observed a fundamental change in American consumption habits. Taking note of the fact that the birth rate moved up and stayed at about 25 per 1,000 in the 1950's, Rostow concluded "Americans

*March 1, 1968.
†Cambridge University Press, 1960.

began to behave as if they preferred the extra baby to the extra unit of consumption." Reading this sentence in the late 1960's one is almost inclined to share the skepticism of John Maynard Keynes on the feasibility of long-range forecasts. In the period of the stepping up of the Vietnam war the birth rate was already declining. In 1967 it was close to the all-time American low of 1932. While this will not affect the annual increase in the labor force based on the high birth rate of the 1950's until early in the 1980's, it is clear that the pressure of employment opportunities resulting from the large numbers of new workers graduating into the labor force will be lessened at that time. This reduces to some extent the required annual rate of growth necessary to maintain full employment. By that time the large influx into urban centers caused by technological unemployment of former farm workers will also have lost the momentum it had in the 1950's and 1960's. This will make it easier to deal with structural unemployment caused by educational deficiencies and lack of work experience.

Technological progress is the other component of the model for economic development. There is no reason to assume that this will not continue. However, while this continuous change has brought about a steady decline in labor requirements as far as physical production is concerned, in the late 1960's there was no evidence that automation of office procedures, especially of data processing, has brought about a decrease in the demand for office workers of all descriptions from highly trained researchers and programmers to keypunch operators. A new type of cost calculus has in fact expanded white-collar employment to the point where it seems to be continuously expanding. It is said that computers are cost effective only if they are in operation on a twenty four hour basis. Like steel mills, offices using computers now must stay open around the clock. This requires a tremendous labor input for programming and a considerable amount of labor for the processing of the information produced by the electronic system. We have seen earlier in this chapter that the share of white-collar workers in total employment, including manufacturing, is continuously increasing. Furthermore, sophisticated office machinery and computers require employees with greater educational achievements. As a result there is a continuous upgrading of job definitions and of their related wage compensations. This tends to increase the aggregate income of nonproduction and production workers and therefore, the scope of discretionary spending, which in turn gives impetus to the demand for goods and services. It is in this prospective that the problem of sustaining growth beyond affluence seems to be open to solutions.

The ever-increasing educational requirements have already led in the United States to a great increase in the enrollment in high school, junior colleges, colleges, and institutions of higher learning. While a considerable part of the school population age 16 and over is according to current practices counted into the labor force because a large number of these students seek part-time employment, there is no doubt that this far greater percentage of the school population is also lessening the pressures on the employment structure. At the same time it increases the demand for teachers and educational administrators on all levels, thereby adding additional employment opportunities.

To sum up: the underlying dynamic situation of the advanced technological system poses problems of economic development of no less complexity than those arising in emerging nations. Specifically in the United States substitutions must be found for public spending for military purposes when and if the international situation would make this feasible. Furthermore, the open-endedness of demand for professional, clerical, and educational personnel adds a new dimension to the labor market. While it is true that an advanced system must be kept on a growth path regardless of already achieved levels of material welfare, continued development is possible if the trends outlined in this section are permitted to come into full operation.

chapter **8**

Problems of Convergence
of Economic Systems

In the first chapter we took a birds-eye view of economic history covering a very large span of time. Seen in this perspective, for long periods of history differentials in the performance of economic systems throughout the world were less apparent than in recent centuries when the Western world entered a period of accelerated economic development. There are striking similarities between the hydraulic state of ancient Egypt and of the irrigation systems of agriculture of the pre-Columbian empires in Central and South America. They shared both a centralized economic administration and a vast pool of unfree labor, and each achieved high standards in construction and in handicrafts. Peasants living in agricultural settings in medieval Europe were close to the economic conditions which formed the frame of reference in many Gospel stories and parables relating to an age more than a thousand years earlier. The rapid pace of economic change associated with the modern age has projected people in advanced systems into an entirely different economic setting, one that renders the down-to-earth stories of the Old and New Testament remote and somewhat unreal, however apt they may have been for a predominantly agricultural economy. The acceleration of economic development in one distinct part of the world, the West, has created an historically unprecedented gap between advanced and retarded countries. It is generally recognized that on a world scale this is an unstable and potentially dangerous situation. The awareness of the perils inherent in this economic development is one of the main reasons why so much attention is paid today to economic assistance for emerging countries, to "nation building," and to efforts to close the gap or at least prevent a further widening.

In the cold-war period following the end of armed conflict in 1945 this basic split between advanced and retarded economies was enhanced by the intrusion of ideologies and the dressing-up of conflicts between world powers as options between utterly different ways of life, root concepts of moral values, and of social and economic organization. The view was very widely held by both parties to the struggle between capitalism and communism that ultimately the world would return to a uniform pattern of economic institutions brought about by the final ascendancy of one system, free enterprise or communism, to the exclusion of the other. Marxism-Leninism maintained for a long period that "monopoly capitalism" was headed toward ever-deepening crises. Even after World War II Stalin asserted that future wars would not be fought between capitalistic countries and the "socialist camp" but between the imperialist powers themselves. Supporters of the abstract concept and the actuality of a free-enterprise system believed in the inevitability of the ultimate failure of the Communist experiment.

The generation that grew up after World War II has witnessed the continued growth without destructive crises of both the "capitalistic" and the Communist system. Far from one system being vanquished or swallowed up by the other, both have continued to develop, to undergo transformations and to coexist rather than to engage in mutual extinction. This recent experience has brought about a considerable change in the thinking about different social-economic systems and their relations in world politics and world markets. As a result, the "adversary type" of approach to economic institutions and development seems to yield to a new concept, the *theory of convergence*. It is asserted that despite their continued ideological and verbal differences, large-scale industrial systems such as the United States and the Common Market countries on the one hand and the economy of the USSR and Eastern countries on the other begin to show considerable similarities on the operational level. From this point of view differences in formal property arrangements, especially the difference between privately and publicly owned large-scale industrial combines are said to be becoming less and less significant because the mode of operation of technologically advanced production systems is dictated by the requirements of technology rather than the exigencies of ownership, whether private or public.

It is necessary to examine the validity of this new theory of convergence in the light of concepts of economic development. To some extent the concrete differences in major industrial systems in the first half of the twentieth century were brought about by the fact that they were not really in the same historical state of economic development. They shared the same astronomical time, but not the same period in terms of their own past history. This is not a total explanation of their conflicts but a further study of this aspect of their stormy relationships from the period of World War I to at least twenty years after World War II will show that underlying many differences was the fact that in the "West" balanced growth was the basic pattern whereas in the "East" unbalanced growth was part of the development design. Such an investigation will be a contribution to the demythologization of economics in which insights provided by a study of the history and structure of economic development will prove useful.

IDEOLOGY AND REALITY IN ECONOMIC DEVELOPMENT

We have seen in our opening chapter that economics as a distinct and systematic scholarly discipline did not arise until the middle of the eighteenth century. It was an intellectual response to the accelerated transformation of a feudalistic, predominantly agricultural system into a much more diversified economy in which commerce and manufacturing played an increasing role. Economic institutions dating back in part many centuries and in part to the more recent policies of mercantilism put unnecessary brakes on the upsurging force of the market. Economics started out as an inquiry into the optimum conditions for the assertion and the free play of these economic forces. One of the early products of systematic economics was the creation of a theoretical model, the free-market system, in which the role of government was confined to the protection of private property and the security of individual persons.

But almost immediately these necessary components of a model for perfect competition were elevated from the levels of economics to broader aspects of a total view of life and of the social institutions designed to protect and to improve the conditions of all individuals linked together in society. The guarantee of private property and of individual security were identified with freedom as such. This freedom was correctly associated with the availability of choices with regard to one's own occupation, profession, business, with one's own preferences concerning consumer goods and saving and spending in general. It was argued that private property—understood in those days primarily as ownership of land, of stocks of trade, or of means of production—was, practically speaking, the indispensable precondition of freedom. On the political plane this was confirmed by the fact that until well into the nineteenth century the right to vote was predicated on the ownership of some property. The expansion of the perfectly competitive model far beyond its immediate application for the purposes of economic analysis was also carried to the all-important problem of social mobility. Early economists rightly denounced still-existing barriers to economic mobility based on social status and class origin. In the aftermath of the French Revolution class privileges were canceled and equality before the law and on the market was granted to all citizens. This being so, it was asserted that a condition of equal opportunities now existed for all people involved in the market situation. It followed that economic success was interpreted as exclusively based on individual initiative, self-reliance, thrift, and industry.

Success or failure in this economic setting were seen as judgments on the inner value of people. Those unable to lift themselves from poverty or low incomes were presumed to be less responsible and less achievement-oriented than those who had come out on top in the competitive struggle of a free market society. The use of the root concepts of private property and individual security beyond the scope of economic theory, their blowing up into a total view of society and of man-linked economic analysis from the very beginning to the social ideology of liberalism. In this way the competitive society in the incipient stage of industrialization—that is, capitalism—was overinterpreted as the guarantee of freedom and as the ultimate phase of progressive economic development. It follows that economic development itself as it occurred in the early part of the nineteenth century was considered the inevitable result of the antecedent structural changes of the market and the almost complete realization of the system of free competition. This being so, the future of individual and political freedom seemed to be predicated on the maintenance of liberalism in all of its political, economic, and individual aspects. The involvement of classical and neoclassical economics in an all-embracing world view of liberalism became virtually complete, as we may learn from one of the most scholarly and comprehensive older texts on economic doctrines. Written by two French authors, Charles Gide and Charles Rist,* this text has been translated into many languages and has gone through many printings, the seventh edition appearing in 1947. Now in this book the whole body of the classical school of economics is combined under the general title "Liberalism." To indicate that this was the leading systematic school of economics, other approaches including Marxism are treated together in another section of the text under the title "The Dissenters." Much later Marxism was referred to by John Maynard Keynes as the "academic underground."

The blending of economic theory with social ideology led to a "one-

---

*C. Gide and C. Rist, *A History of Economic Doctrines,* Boston, Heath, 1947.

way only" concept of economic development. The idea gained hold that if there is to be economic development at all it must follow the pattern established by Western capitalism, extending itself into the rest of the world by foreign investment, in international trade and in the acquisition of colonies. Thus when after World War I an entirely different social pattern of economic development was started in the USSR, the issue was not debated on either side in terms of requirements inherent in different phases and real targets of economic development, but as options between inalterably opposed ultimate values and interpretations of society and of the world. The ideology of economic liberalism almost inevitably brought forth the counterideology of socialism. Because liberalism had claimed too much, it was easy for early critics of the system to point to great inequalities which, far from having been removed by the repeal of legal restrictions and inhibitions, seemed to be growing worse as industrialization spread under the institutional forms of private property of means of production. Now, just as liberalism had established a link between individual freedom and private property, socialism as a counterideology insisted that it was precisely this type of private property that perpetuated inequality and prevented the ever-increasing class of industrial workers from sharing in the fruits of economic development. In fact, economic progress was viewed as being achieved under capitalism by exploiting in its first phases the domestic working class of industrial countries and in later stages the inhabitants of colonial and underdeveloped areas of the world. Hence in logical contradiction to liberalism, socialism maintained that the emancipation of the masses and the access to equal opportunity—and therefore freedom—demanded the abolition of private property and its conversion into social ownership.

The reality of the development of capitalism and of socialism has shown that the ideological claims of either system are unfounded. The basic reason for this gap between ideology and reality is to be found in the original overextension of purely economic analysis into a total system claiming to be a prescription for a perfect society. Actually the least valid distinction between these two ideologies would be that between "idealism" and "materialism" or between "individualism" and "collectivism." Both share the view that economic structures and conditions are of decisive influence on all other aspects of society. Seen in this context, the difference is rather one between the "praxis" or de facto materialism of liberalism and materialism as a theory of socialism, or on the human level between individual and collective standardization and conformism as requirements of work adjustment to modern production systems and business and administrative procedures become more stringent. In the later part of the twentieth century a more mature view begins to take hold. It now can be seen far more clearly that actual economic development has supported neither the noneconomic pretensions of capitalism nor those of socialism. In fact, in the course of economic development itself both systems have undergone basic changes. Before we discuss them in the light of the theory of convergence, it is necessary to study in some detail these changes within capitalism and socialism. Both have undergone great structural alterations which to a certain extent were affected by their mutual influences on each other. Only if these aspects of their development are clearly understood will it be possible to evaluate the theory of convergence and to redefine the real differences in these systems.

TRANSFORMATIONS IN CAPITALISM AND SOCIALISM

In our study of the accelerated development of such highly industrialized countries as West Germany and Japan and in our analysis of the structural changes that occur in a system which already has achieved affluence but is compelled to continue its forward momentum, we have already encountered many factors that have radically transformed the actual capitalist system. While the institutions of private property have been maintained, there is now little resemblance to the original simple model of a free-enterprise system.

This can be clearly seen in the changes of the profit system itself. Profits are still considered the main motivating force for continued expansion and improvements of the capitalistic system. However, up until recently profits were considered primarily a form of the income of natural or "real" persons. Often they were called entrepreneutrial income. Today in the United States and in other advanced countries profits largely accrue not to natural but to legal "persons," and to business corporations. In this sense the profit system has changed from an individualistic to a collectivistic arrangement. This is clearly seen also in the fact that in the American practice, dividend payments to individual stockholders in the average account for only half of the corporate profits after taxes.

Corporate property is private but certainly not individual in nature. It is true that in a legal sense stockholders have a claim to a small fraction of this property but this fact has no bearing on the actual operations or on the decision-making procedures of private enterprise. Decision making itself has become a complex procedure encompasing many stages and requiring the service of a considerable number of professionally trained employees. While in any system of management the personal characteristics and abilities of the top executives are often of considerable though undefinable significance, modern business methods depend on team management rather than our "lonely decisions" of the chief executive of a corporation. A good organization requires that top management is free from the burdens of day-to-day decisions and can dedicate itself to a continuous review of the broad aspects of the operations of the enterprise. The rigidly enforced rules of compulsory retirement in American corporations also has brought about comparatively short terms of office of top decision makers and a healthy rotation among job holders in the highest echelons of big business. In a way the corporation itself develops a collective personality of its own. At all times it looms larger than any individuals who occupy the front offices at any given time.

The leadership personnel in such an advanced system, especially in the United States, moves frequently from the public to the private sector, and vice versa. The government, far from exercising only minimum functions on a free-market system, is actually all present within the economic structure. Even if there should be an exchange within government expenditures between military and civilian appropriations to the advantage of the latter, the close interrelations between the governmental and the corporate structures will not change essentially.

The individual-enterprise system of early capitalism has been modified into a structure of private collectivism in which the public sector assumes a large role. However, the capitalist system has not only been transformed from individual to collective private property and from personal to collective decision making, but the original class structure—placing profit-making property owners on one side and propertyless workers on the other—has become blurred. The line of demarcation today between various groups of the population does not lie along the structure of property but rather is determined by distinctions between the various levels of management—higher, middle and lower ranks of executives, and wage and salary earners. In the latter group additional distinctions had developed between highly skilled and less skilled workers and between organized and unorganized labor. Most important is the elimination of much of the early instability of the capitalist system through the setting up of various forms of social insurance. Very significantly executive employees share in the benefits of these public systems with other wage and salary workers. The encouragement of collective bargaining has raised the bargaining power and the income of organized labor; indirectly through the spillover effect it has also increased the earnings of those who are not part of organized labor.

To sum up: since socialism emerged as a counterideology to economic liberalism the capitalist system which it claimed it would supersede in the long run has changed beyond recognition. It has become more collectivist, more stable, and has succeeded in including vast proportions of the wage and salary earners in the prosperity sector of the economy.

We now turn to a brief study of the transformations of socialism. The problem here differs from capitalism in one important respect: the development of capitalism from an individual enterprise structure to private collectivism was going on while an actual business system corresponding more or less to the perfectly competitive model of economic theory was operative. In a way it can be said that liberal economic theory followed with a certain time lag the development of a market society. Facts preceded theory so far as capitalism is concerned. In socialism, theory came before facts. While classical Marxism expected the inevitable transformation of the capitalist system into a socialist system, nothing of that kind happened when socialism was superimposed on the disorganized and backward economy of Russia after World War I. Because Marx's *Capital* is an analysis of capitalism and its alleged laws of development, it did not contain any guidelines for the setting up of a socialist economy. In fact, Lenin and other writers pointed out prior to the seizure of power in Russia that capitalism itself was making workers ready for socialism by training them to be efficient and productive and by developing managerial methods that could be taken over by socialist enterprises.

As we have seen in Chapter 5, absolute priority was given in the USSR to the building up of heavy industries and of social overhead capital to the neglect of agriculture and the consumer sector. Far from benefiting from an advanced stage of capitalistic development in Russia itself, in the 1920's and 1930's the Soviet Union was compelled to employ foreign engineers and to import capital equipment while struggling to educate an inefficient first generation of industrial workers. Socialism, when it was still a counterideology rather than an established system, had asserted that while under capitalism production was for profits, under socialism it was for the satisfaction of human needs. It soon became clear that this goal was interpreted by the Soviet leaders on a collective rather than on an individual basis. The needs turned out to be the needs of society rather than those of individual consumers. Consumers good production above and beyond the essentials necessary to maintain worker efficiency had to be postponed for more than a generation in the Soviet Union.

It should be stressed that these differences do not of itself prove the superiority of capitalism over socialism. When the Russian Revolution got under way after World War I the condition of the working class in Europe and in the United States began to improve very rapidly. But two generations earlier industrial workers in the early stages of capitalism were also limited to a near-subsistence level of living in the Western World. The comparative prosperity of workers under capitalism in the early twentieth century and poverty of Russian workers under socialism was not so much the result of basic differences between the systems but of different phases of economic development. These differences also played a large role in the consumer sector. Czarist Russia had not placed much emphasis on the development of consumer goods industries, whereas in Europe and the United States small enterprises had been operative over a long period of time prior to the industrial revolution in the production of a large variety of consumer goods. It was not until about forty years after the start of the Bolshevik Revolution and ten years after the end of World War II that greater attention was given to the "human needs" of the Russian consumers. Only then was there a stepping up of residential building construction and of the output of consumer goods. Up to this point Soviet planners had a right to assume that because of deliberately engineered scarcities of consumer goods, whatever would be produced for personal consumption would automatically be purchased by Russian householders. Suddenly a phenomenon inconsistent with previous operative concepts of socialism developed in the Soviet Union: unsold merchandise began to pile up on the shelves of retail outlets and in warehouses. Even a slight improvement in the real income of consumers made them more discriminating. They insisted on better quality, greater variety, and more attractive design of items for personal use and consumption. For decades the Soviet system had emphasized the priority of the quantity of output over quality. Now it became apparent that purely quantitative yardsticks were inadequate in an economy whose production potential was steadily rising and in which the consumer sector was permitted to grow with the increase in the national product. It is in this connection that profit considerations had to be introduced into Soviet economic practices.

Actually almost from the beginning material incentives through piece-work compensations and bonuses had been employed in the Soviet economy in order to stimulate the efficiency of labor and of management. However, this type of premium pay was tied strictly to the quantity of production, especially to an exceeding of production norms. This method proved to be self-defeating once the focus shifted from quantity to quality of production. A transformation took place in the old structure of the consumer-goods industry in the Soviet Union.

This change had two aspects. The first was a redefinition of the yardsticks for bonuses which could be earned by enterprises and distributed to management and to labor. Instead of using output criteria, a profit concept was introduced. Under this new system the bonuses were given for maximizing sales revenues through the device of lowering cost rather than increasing production. The intention of this change was to penalize enterprises and especially managers if they continued their former practices of hoarding unnecessary labor and raw materials merely in order to meet contingencies in the race for output quotas. Furthermore, this new bonus system was designed to encourage experimentation with new production methods which under the old system had often been rejected in order not to lose out on production goals.

The second aspect of the change was the establishment of a direct link between consumer-goods industries and retail outlets. This eliminated a great deal of centralized planning concerning the design and quality and even quantity of consumer goods. By dealing directly with manufacturers, Soviet retailers now can order what they think is being demanded by consumers. On the other hand, consumer-goods manufacturers do compete to a certain extent among themselves for orders to be placed by the retail trade.

This transformation certainly does not entitle us to conclude that the socialist system has adopted a capitalistic profit structure. But it has opened the road to a greater emphasis on the market and has pointed the way toward an increase in the "market socialism" sector within the Communist economic system.

We have seen that in a way capitalism has become more collectivist, and that communism has become somewhat more individualist. We will inquire now what all this means in the light of a theory of convergence.

The original doctrine of Marxism-Leninism anticipated ever more severe crises in the capitalist system during which pauperization would spread from the working class upward to reach formerly independent proprietors who could not survive in the competitive struggle with more efficient large-scale capitalist enterprises. This forecast anticipated a polarization of the economic society with few, exceedingly wealthy and powerful capitalists on the one hand and an ever-increasing mass of poor workers and former middle-class people on the other. Actually the development has been exactly in the opposite direction. The middle classes, far from joining the proletariat, have been joined in their way of life and standard of living by skilled organized blue-collar labor and the vast bulk of wage and salary earners who are regularly employed. It should be stressed that in the *Communist Manifesto* the industrial workers were presented as making up the proletariat, whereas groups which we would classify today as marginal or peripheral workers or even as "unemployables" were called in the same basic document of Communism the ' proletariat in rags" (*Lumpenproletariat*). It is interesting to note that the proletarian working class was expected to be the basis for the formation of the "advance guard" or Communist party leading the rest of society to socialism and communism. The proletarians in rags were said to be more likely to support right-wing dictatorships. But the "classical" proletariat of industrial workers no longer exists. It has been integrated into the prosperity sector of society and has become status quo minded. Far from being an economic or social "underclass," it has entered the main stream of middle-class society.

The transformation of the capitalist system into a welfare state and of the communist system into a stable structure in which real incomes are rising and scientific, technical, managerial and other leading positions are proliferating has brought actual ways of life of people in the United States and USSR much closer than was anticipated either by the proponents of Marxism or the advocates of classical capitalism.

On the ideological plane the formerly monolithic thought structure of Marxism was already punctured under Stalin when he formulated the goal of "catching up and surpassing capitalism." Khrushchev committed the error of naming specific dates at which this surpassing of the American economy was to take place. In our context it does not matter too much that the Soviet Union is still lagging far behind the United States. However, the trends of the past ten years indicate that independent of purely statistical comparisons of the GNP which are of problematical validity, middle-class ways of life long predominant in the United States are spreading in the USSR. The reasons for this convergence will be discussed in greater detail in the next section.

THE REAL BASIS OF CONVERGENCE

In our study of the real as distinct from the ideological aspects of economic development and of the transformations within capitalism as well as within socialism, we have concluded that an abstract-model approach to these problems does not come to grips with the nature of the changes during this period of accelerated advance in economic activities all over the world. The actual course of events has taken much of the substance out of the old controversy between individualistic capitalism and collectivist socialism. It has particularly refuted the Marxist doctrine that the property arrangements surrounding production systems are absolutely decisive for the structure of society, the relations between various groups participating in the economic process and on a more general level the prevailing ideas in society. A study of the transformations which have occurred in capitalism and socialism in the past fifty years has shown that there are other factors which are far more important than formal ownership relations which bring about fundamental structural changes in the operational concepts and management of a highly industralized system. The convergence of advanced economic systems noted by many analysists is not on the level of ideologies that are still being promulgated within the two systems as though they were relevant. But behind the veil of old-line verbalizations according to the stereotypes of free enterprise and socialism, a new reality is emerging which asserts itself independent of the legal and economic concepts prevailing in a particular economic system. John Kenneth Galbraith,* the coiner of some words that have become part of the American idiom, has called this complex the "technostructure." We will use this concept in order to clarify further the real scope and meaning of the convergence of advanced economic systems. We will then find that it is not the property order as such but the requirements of large-scale industrial systems of production which shape in a decisive manner the operational processes of an economic system. This also will bring out the fact that convergence is not a compromise between formerly diametrically opposed ideas but a trend toward greater similarity in actual economic and social systems of highly advanced countries.

The tendency toward ever larger units of production is required by the exigencies of progressive technology. We have seen in Chapter 5 that this applies also to agriculture. But the main impact of this steady advance in mechanization and automation is on the size of the industrial production unit. Now this imposes an organizational form on enterprises which will assert itself regardless of the prevailing ideologies.

Highly advanced industrial systems require managerial skills which in turn can be acquired only by intensive study and training and experience in service with the operation of such systems. Just as the "capitalistic enterprise" of vast scale is too complex and too sensitive to be left in its management to the accident of personal inheritance of a member of an owner family, the socialist counterpart of such an enterprise is not being exposed to the assignment of managers on a purely political level. In both systems professional managers will prevail. They will be close to the politi-

---

*J. K. Galbraith, *The New Industrial State,* Boston, Houghton, 1967.

cal power structure in each system, although in both top leadership in state and party or parties is most likely to go to the people who have been full-time professionals in politics rather than in economics for a considerable period of time.

Modern complex production systems require sophisticated procedures such as data processing and linear programming. Continued basic research is necessary in order to keep operations consistent with new developments in science and technology. Hence in addition to the professional managers of production, highly skilled, scientifically trained personnel are needed in order to keep the enterprises and industries updated or to upgrade their operations to new levels of efficiency consistent the progress of methods of production.

It is this type of enterprise that accounts for a large proportion of the labor force employed in manufacturing, and continuous upgrading takes place even on the production worker level. The share of skilled workers is continuously increasing and the demand for undereducated or untrained workers is declining. The high productivity of large-scale enterprises makes manpower resources available for other lines of work. A simultaneous increase in office and in service employment is noticeable as output in agriculture and industry increases while labor requirements in these basic sectors of the economy are declining.

Because high-output operations require experienced, well-trained management, a sharp line of demarcation is maintained in both systems between the executive branch of the enterprise and the blue-and white-collar employees. Outside the production sectors of such an advanced economy educational structures are continuously expanding in order to supply modern industry and government and science with manpower of high academic achievements. More people and resources are also constantly made available for the development of purely cultural activities.

In such advanced systems class origin becomes less important than performance scores in schools and in work settings. As the society becomes more open and provides greater opportunities for upward mobility, a restructuring of social groupings takes place in which people share similar educational backgrounds, comparable incomes, and equivalent social functions. Rigid class distinctions yield to social differentiations according to more flexible lines in which education and economic and social job identifications play a more important role. In this respect the United States and the USSR have somewhat more in common between themselves than they have with Western European countries. In the United States, which has always been a predominantly middle class society, class barriers as distinct from race barriers were less rigid than in the old European countries. In the Soviet Union the Communist Revolution deliberately destroyed the old social classes, often by inflicting great hardships on members of former ruling groups through expropriation and exile. But there is no doubt that fifty years of Communist rule, while they have not created economic equality or an equalitarian society, have certainly made great progress toward greater social mobility, thereby widening the opportunities for ascendance to higher social roles and incomes within this system. Although Western European countries have also moved in this direction, their long background in more or less rigid class societies has preserved to a greater extent class distinction as a state of mind than is the case in the United States or in the Soviet Union.

Another powerful factor for convergence is that property is no longer the dividing line between various classes of society. We have already seen that a much more meaningful division has evolved both in the United States and in the Soviet Union between those groups of the labor force who work in an executive, managerial, professional, and executive capacity and those who are carrying out operations and production plans as wage and salary earners. The new middle classes which have emerged on such a vast scale in the United States and which are increasing in significance in the Soviet Union are in a position to purchase a large number of durable consumer goods. Home building for individual families has recently been encouraged even in the Soviet Union and, contrary to opinions voiced by Khrushchev, mass production of low-priced automobiles has gotten under way in the USSR by licensing the Fiat Company of Italy. But this middle-class status is determined by economic function and income and is not connected as it had been originally to the ownership of land and of business property. Middle-class ways cover more and more of advanced industrial society no matter what the formal structure of property is. What is emerging, however, is a more or less affluent but basically propertyless middle class.

It should be noted that convergence has been viewed here strictly as an economic, technological, and managerial process with its implications for the social structure. As such, this type of development is neutral toward and independent of ultimate value commitments. Nor does this high level of economic achievement solve all other social problems. In fact it has made racial conflict within advanced countries and in their relation to the rest of the world more serious and threatening. It is one of the great limitations and shortcomings of the Marxist theory of economic development to have asserted that once property and production problems had been solved all sources of conflict between individuals and between various groups of society—or for that matter between nations—had been effectively eliminated. One of the most important lessons of the twentieth century has been that economic progress, which has been so spectacular especially after the half-century mark is not a total problem-solving procedure.

This is shown clearly in the international unrest which spread both in the East and in the West among the younger generation involved in higher studies at universities and colleges in the 1960's. The technostructure so highly successful in maintaining the forward momentum of advanced systems requires a great deal of personal adjustment, achievement, and identification. This open-ended economic development threatens, however, to lead to a monolithic, closed system of a completely industrialized civilization in which the vital space for individual growth and development seems to be narrowing to a degree that is unacceptable to many, especially the ever-increasing number of highly educated young people. But at this point the problem ceases to be economic and becomes instead social, psychological, and philosophical. The higher the degree of economic development, the more urgent becomes problem of meta-economics.

THE REMAINING DANGERS OF DIVERGENCE
IN DEVELOPMENT

In Chapter 4 we stressed that one of the paradoxes of economic development is the fact that the gap between advanced and emerging nations is threatening to widen as highly advanced countries continue along the lines of accelerated growth, whereas in retarded economy resources grow less rapidly than population pressures. At a time when the world seemed to be split into two irreconcilable power structures, one capitalist and the other socialist, there was great danger that this conflict would project itself into the whole problem of economic development on an international scale. In fact, in the 1950's a struggle developed for the allegience to one or the other bloc of the newly decolonized nations of the world. While there too is much combustible material spread around the world to permit an entirely optimistic appraisal, the de facto convergence industrial structures of the superpowers has led to the conviction that they have nothing to gain from military conflict among themselves. But this and the tendency toward convergence do not eliminate the threat imposed by the widening gap between highly advanced and underdeveloped nations.

Originally Marxism was international in a very specific sense. Using the one-dimensional analytical scheme of historical materialism, it assumed that the solidarity of the working classes would prove to be stronger than middle-class nationalism. Even Lenin during and immediately after World War I was still of the opinion that the Communist Revolution in Russia would soon be followed by a similar takeover of power by the proletariat in the industrial countries of Europe. Nothing of the kind happened. Leon Trotsky, the close associate of Lenin in the early years of the Bolshevik revolution, pressed for an international permanent revolution in the 1920's but was crushed by Stalin, who developed the concepts of the building up of "Socialism in One Country"—the Soviet Union, of course.

The wide gap in levels of development and the vast differences in world standards of living throughout the world with two-thirds of the world population living in underdeveloped countries have led to a latter-day revival of a modified Marxist concept of the international class struggle. Now it is conceived not as an ultimate confrontation between industrial workers and capitalists in advanced countries but between land-less farm populations and land-owners, and generally between highly developed "neocolonialist" countries and the majority of mankind which does not share on a mass basis in the benefits of contemporary economic development.

The art of leadership consists largely in anticipation of the course of events and in keeping abreast of them and in retaining at all times the initiative. A study of the history and structure of economic development is a necessary tool in the exercise of this high type of political activity. To perpetuate divisions of ideology policy and politics which have their roots in the nineteenth century instead of embarking on broader efforts to strengthen international economic development on a broad front would be an invitation to disaster for both capitalism and socialism. It would be a threat to the very real economic progress that has been achieved under both systems in the last few decades.

Bibliography

CHAPTER 1

A Bird's-Eye View of Economic Development

Gill Richard T., *Economic Development: Past and Present,* Prentice-Hall, 1967.

Herskovits, Melville J., *Economic Anthropology,* Norton, 1940.

Hoselitz, Bert F., *Theories of Economic Growth,* Free Press, 1960.

Meier, Gerald M., and Robert E. Baldwin, *Economic Development: Theory, History, Policy,* Wiley, 1957.

Peet, T. E., *The Stone and Bronze Ages in Italy and Sicily,* 1909.

Rostovtzev, Michael, *The Social and Economic History of the Roman Empire,* Oxford U. P., 1957.

Levy, Jean-Philippe, *The Economic Life of the Ancient World,* trans. by John G. Biram, U. of Chicago Press, 1967.

Heichelheim, F. M., *An Ancient Economic History,* trans. by J. Stevens, Leyden, 1958.

Approaches to Economic Development

Galbraith, John Kenneth, *Economic Development in Perspective,* Harvard U. P., 1962.

Higgins, Benjamin, *Economic Development: Principles, Problems, Policies,* rev. ed., Norton, 1968.

Jackson, Barbara (Ward), *The Rich Nations and the Poor Nations,* Norton, 1962.

Leibenstein, Harvey, *Economic Backwardness and Economic Growth,* Wiley, 1957.

Lewis, W. Arthur, *The Theory of Economic Growth,* Irwin, 1955.

List, Friedrich, *The National System of Political Economy,* Kelley, 1966.

Mill, John Stuart, *Principles of Political Economy*, Longmans, 1867.

Myrdal, Gunnar, *Rich Lands and Poor*, Harper, 1957.

————, *Asian Drama, An Inquiry into the Poverty of Nations*, Twentieth Century Fund, 1968.

Novack, David E., and Robert Lekachman, *Development and Society*, St. Martin's 1964,

Okun, Bernard, and Richard W. Richardson, *Studies in Economic Development*, Holt, 1961.

Parsons, Talcott, and Neil J. Smelser, *Economy and Society*, Free Press, 1965.

Ricardo, David, *The Principles of Political Economy and Taxation*, Bell, 1891.

Schumpeter, Joseph, *The Theory of Economic Development*, trans. by Revers Opie, Harvard U. P., 1934.

Singer, Hans W., *International Development: Growth and Change*, McGraw–Hill, 1964.

Strosslin, Werner, *Friedrich List's Lehre von der wirtschaflichen Entwicklung*, Mohr, 1968.

Villard, Henry H., *Economic Development*, Holt, 1959.

Population

Appleman, Philip, *The Silent Explosion*, Beacon, 1955.

Barclay, George W., *The Technique of Population Analysis*, Wiley, 1958.

Belshaw, Horace, *Population Growth and Levels of Consumption*, Institute of Pacific Relations, 1956.

Bennett, Merrill Kelley, *The World's Food*, Harper, 1954.

Beshers, James M., *Population Processes in Social Systems*, Free Press, 1967.

Brown, Harrison S., *The Challenge of Man's Future*, Viking, 1954.

Coons, Carelton S., *The Story of Man*, Knopf, 1955.

Carr-Saunders, Alexander Morris, *World Population: Past Growth and Present Trends*, Clarendon, 1936.

Cepede, Michel, *Population and Food*, Sheed and Ward, 1964.

Coale, Ansley J. and Edgar M. Hoover, *Population Growth and Economic Development in Low Income Countries*, Princeton U. P. 1958.

Davis, Kingsley, *The Population of India and Pakistan*, Princeton U. P. 1958.

Forde, C. Daryl, *Habitat, Economy and Society*, Dutton, 1952.

Francis, Roy G., *The Population Ahead*, U. of Minnesota Press, 1958.

Hauser, Philip M., *Population and World Politics*, Free Press, 1958.

Hertzler, Joyce O., *Crisis in World Population,* U. of Nebraska Press, 1956.

Leibenstein, Harvey, *A Theory of Demographic Development,* Princeton U. P. 1954.

Mair, George F. (ed.), *Studies in Population,* Princeton U. P., 1949.

Malthus T. R., *An Essay on the Principle of Population,* Johnson, 1903.

Peterson, William, *Population,* Macmillan, 1961.

Smith, T. E., "The Cocos-Keeling Islands: A Demographic Laboratory," *Population Studies* 14:2 (November 1960) pp. 94-138.

Smith, T. Lynn, *Population Analysis,* McGraw-Hill, 1948.

Spengler, J. J., "Economic Factors in the Development of Densely Populated Areas," *Proceedings of the American Philosophical Society,* 1951.

Stamp, Dudley, *Our Developing Planet,* Faber, 1960.

Stuart, Alexander J., *Overpopulation: Twentieth Century Nemesis,* Exposition, 1958.

Thomlinson, Ralph, *Population Dynamics,* Random, 1965.

United Nations Department of Economic and Social Affairs, "The Future Growth of World Population," *Population Studies* 2:28 (1958).

Vogt, William, *People: Challenge to Survival,* Sloane, 1960.

CHAPTER 2

Unfree Labor

Abdy, John Thomas, *Feudalism: Its Rise, Progress and Consequences,* Bell, 1890.

Barrow, G., *Feudal Britain,* Arnold, 1956.

Barrow, R. H., *Slavery in the Roman Empire,* Dial, 1928.

Bell, Andrew, *Historical Sketches of Feudalism,* Partridge and Oakey, 1852.

Block, Marc Leopold Benjamin, *Feudal Society,* trans. by L. A. Manyon, U. of Chicago Press, 1964.

Conrad, Alfred H., *The Economics of Slavery,* Aldine, 1964.

Coulborn, Rushton (ed.), *Feudalism in History,* Anchor, 1965.

Davis, William Sterns, *Life on a Mediaeval Barony,* Harper 1923.

Duff, Arnold Mackay, *Freedman in the Early Roman Empire,* Clarendon, 1958.

Finley, Moses I., *Slavery in Classical Antiquity,* Heffer, 1960.

Flanders, Ralph Betts, *Plantation Slavery in Georgia,* Edwards, 1967.

Freyre, Gilberto, *The Masters and the Slaves,* trans. by Samuel Putnam, Knopf, 1964.

Ganshof, François Louis, *Feudalism,* trans. by Phillip Griesson, Longmans, 1964.

Gibbs, Marion, *Feudal Order,* Schuman, 1953.

Glotz, Gustave, *Ancient Greece at Work,* Knopf, 1926.

Jernegan, Marcus Wilson, *Laboring and Dependent Classes in Colonial America,* U. of Chicago Press, 1931.

Link, Edith (Murr), *The Emancipation of the Austrian Peasant,* Columbia U. P., 1949.

Lyon, Bryce Dale, *From Fief to Indenture,* Harvard U. P. 1957.

Mathieson, William Law, *Great Britain and the Slave Trade,* Octagon, 1967.

Painter, Sidney, *The Rise of Feudal Monarchies,* Cornell U. P., 1960.

Patterson, Orlando, *The Sociology of Slavery,* MacGibbon and Kee, 1967.

Petit-Dutaillis, Charles Edmond, *The Feudal Monarchy in France and England from the Tenth to the Thirteenth Centuries,* Kegan Paul, 1936.

Phillips, Ulrich Bannell, *Life and Labor in the Old South,* Grosset, 1929.

Seignobos, Charles, *The Feudal Regime,* trans. by Earl W. Dow, Holt, 1929.

Stenton, Sir Frank Merry, *The First Century of English Feudalism,* 1066-1166, 2d ed., Clarendon, 1961.

Stephenson, Carl, *Mediaeval Feudalism,* Cornell U. P. 1942.

Strayer, Joseph Reese, *Feudalism,* Van Nostrand, 1965.

Ullman, Walter, *The Individual and Society in the Middle Ages,* Johns Hopkins, 1966.

Westermann, William Linn, *The Slave Systems of Greek and Roman Antiquity,* American Philosophical Society, 1955.

Williams, Eric, *Capitalism and Slavery,* U. of North Carolina Press, 1944.

Woodman, Harold D. (ed.), *Slavery and the Southern Economy,* Harcourt, 1966.

Zavala, Silvio Arturo, *The Defense of Human Rights in Latin America,* UNESCO, 1964.

Economic History of The Middle Ages

Block, Marc Leopold Benjamin, *Lord and Worker in Medieval Europe,* trans. by J. E. Anderson, U. of California Press, 1967.

The Cambridge Economic History: Vol. I, *The Agrarian Life of the Middle Ages,* 1941; Vol. II, *Trade and Industry in the Middle Ages,* (1953); Vol. III, *Economic Organization and Policies in the Middle Ages,* 1963.

Latouche, Robert *The Birth of Western Democracy,* trans. by E. M. Wilkinson, Barnes and Noble, 1961.

Pirenne, Henri, *Economic and Social History of Medieval Europe,* Kagan Paul, 1936.

Thompson, James Westfall, *An Economic and Social History of the Middle Ages,* Century, 1920.

Accumulation of Labor

Oppenheimer, Franz, *The State,* Vanguard, 1928.

Latin America

Bannon, John Francis, S.J., *Latin America: An Historical Survey,* 2d ed., Bruce, 1963.

Chapman, Charles E., *Colonial Hispanic America,* Macmillan, 1933.

Chevalier, François, *Land and Society in Colonial Mexico,* U. of California Press, 1963.

Diffie, Bailey Wallys, *Latin American Civilization: Colonial Period,* Stackpole, 1945.

Flores, Edmundo "Land Reform and the Alliance for Progress," in Laura Randall (ed.), "Economic Development: Evolution or Revolution?," *Studies in Economics,* 1964.

Haring, Clarence Henry, *The Spanish Empire in America,* Oxford U. P., 1947.

Hawthorne, Julian, *Spanish America: From the Earliest Period to the Present Time,* Collier, 1901.

Herring, Hubert Clinton, *A History of Latin America from the Beginning to the Present,* 2d ed., Knopf, 1961.

Madariaga, Salvador de, *The Rise of the Spanish American Empire,* Macmillan, 1947.

————, *The Fall of the Spanish American Empire,* Hollis and Carter, 1947.

Moore, David Richard, *A History of Latin America,* Prentice-Hall, 1942.

CHAPTER 3

Economic Development

Adelman, Irma, *The Theory and Design of Economic Development,* Johns Hopkins and Center for Agricultural and Economic Development, Iowa State University, 1966.

Agarwala, Amar Narain, *The Economies of Underdevelopment,* Oxford U. P., 1958.

Alexander, Robert Jackson, *A Primer of Economic Development,* Macmillan, 1962.

Alpert, Paul, *Economic Development: Objectives and Methods,* Free Press, 1963.

Baldwin, Robert E., *Economic Development and Growth,* Wiley, 1966.

Bauer, Peter Tamas, *The Economics of Underdeveloped Countries,* U. of Chicago Press, 1962.

Bonne, Alfred, *Studies in Economic Development,* Kegan Paul, 1957.

Brookings Institute, Washington D.C., *Development of the Emerging Countries,* 1962.

Bruton, Henry J., *Principles of Development Economics,* Prentice-Hall, 1965.

Buchanan, Norman S., and Howard S. Ellis, *Approaches to Economic Development,* Twentieth Century Fund, 1955.

Dillard, Dudley, *Economic Development of the North Atlantic Community,* Prentice-Hall, 1967.

Gill, Richard T., *Economic Development: Past and Present,* Prentice-Hall, 1967.

Hirschman, Albert O., *The Strategy of Economic Development,* Yale U. P., 1958.

_____, *Journey Toward Progress,* Twentieth Century Fund, 1963.

CHAPTER 4

Inflation

Bach, George Leland, *Inflation,* Brown U. P., 1958.

Baker, Clayton, *Depression and Inflation,* Vantage, 1963.

Chandler, Lester Vernon, *Inflation in the United States, 1940-1948,* Harper, 1951.

Clark, John Maurice, *How to Check Inflation,* Public Affairs Committee, 1942.

Clifford, Arthur Morton, *In the Grip of Inflation,* 1947.

Fellner, William John, et al., *The Problem of Rising Prices,* Organization for European Economic Cooperation, 1961.

Haberler, Gottfried, *Inflation,* American Enterprise Institute for Public Policy Research, 1966.

Hardy, Charles O., K. B. Williams, and H. S. Ellis, *Prices, Wages and Employment,* Washington Board of Governors of The Federal Reserve System, 1946.

Palzi, Melchior, *An Inflation Primer,* Regnery, 1961.

Schultz, Charles L., *Recent Inflation in the United States,* Joint Economic Committee of the Congress of the United States, Study Paper No. 1, 1959.

Samuelson, Paul, *Economics; An Introductory Analysis,* 7th ed., McGraw-Hill, 1967, Chap. 15.

Steiner, Peter O. and Richard Liprey, *Economics,* Harper, 1966, Chap. 58.

Approaches to Economic Development

See the same category at end of Chapter 1.

Income and Employment

United States Department Of Labor, *Manpower Reports of The President,* 1962-67.

CHAPTER 5

Agriculture and Economics

Bishop, Charles E., *Introduction to Agricultural Economic Analysis,* Wiley, 1958.

Boserup, Ester, *The Conditions of Economic Growth,* Allen and Unwin, 1965.

Chang, P'ei-kang, *Agriculture and Industrialization,* Harvard U. P., 1949.

Cohen, Ruth Louise, *The Economics of Agriculture,* rev. ed., Pitman, 1949.

Eicher, Carl, (ed.), *Agriculture in Economic Development,* McGraw-Hill, 1964.

Hibbard, Benjamin Horace, *Agricultural Economics,* McGraw-Hill, 1948.

Ojala, E., *Agriculture and Economic Progress,* Oxford U. P., 1952.

Schultz, Theodore W., *Transforming Traditional Agriculture,* Yale U. P., 1964.

CHAPTER 6

Japanese Economic Development

Allen, G. C., *Japan's Economic Recovery,* Oxford U. P., 1958.

————, *Japan's Economic Expansion,* Oxford U. P., 1965.

Ayusawa, Iwao F., *A History of Labor in Modern Japan*, East-West Center Press, 1966.

Broadbridge, Seymour, *Industrial Dualism In Japan*, Cass, 1966.

Cohen, Jerome B., *Japan's Postwar Economy*, Indiana U. P., 1958.

Cowan, C. D., *The Economic Development of China and Japan*, Praeger, 1964.

Dore, R. P., *Land Reform in Japan*, Oxford U. P., 1959.

Komiya, Ryutaro (ed.), *Postwar Economic Growth in Japan*, trans. by Robert S. Ozaki, U. of California Press, 1966.

Kuznets, Simon, Wilbert E. Moore, and Joseph J. Spengler, *Economic Growth: Brazil, India, Japan*, Duke U. P., 1955.

Lockwood, William W., *The Economic Development of Japan*, Princeton U. P., 1954.

German Economic Development

Jacoby, Neil H., and James E. Howell, *European Economies East and West*, World, 1967.

Lamfulussy, A., *The United Kingdom and the Six*, Irwin, 1963.

Maddison, Angus, *Economic Growth in the West*, Norton, 1964.

Roepke, Wilhelm, *A Humane Economy*, Regnery, 1960.

Wilcox, Clair, Willis D. Weatherford, Halland Hunter, and Morton S. Baratz, *Economies of the World Today*, Harcourt, 1966.

CHAPTER 7

The Theory of Convergence

Azrael, Jeremy, *Managerial Power and Soviet Politics*, Harvard U. P., 1966.

Burnham, James, *The Managerial Revolution*, Indiana U. P., 1960.

Drucker, Peter, *The New Society*, Harper, 1962.

Galbraith, John Kenneth, *The New Industrial State*, Houghton, 1967.

Granick, David, *The Red Executive*, Doubleday, 1960.

Heilbroner, Robert L., *The Limits of American Capitalism*, Harper, 1966.

Richman, Barry, *Management, Development and Education in The Soviet Union*, Michigan State University International Business Studies, 1967.

Salisbury, Harrison E., *The Soviet Union: The Fifty Years*, Harcourt, 1967.

Schwartz, Harry, *Russia and the Soviet Economy*, Prentice-Hall, 1963.

Tinbergen, Jan, "Do Communist and Free Economies Show a Convergence Pattern?" *Soviet Studies,* April 1961.

Turgeon, Lynn, *The Contrasting Economies: A Study of Modern Economic Systems,* Allyn and Bacon, 1963.

Index

Military establishment, 157
Military hardware, 158
Mill, John Stuart, 8, 9
Mining industry, 136
    support of, 137
Mississippi Company, 83
Mixed economy, 138
Monetary policies, 152
Monnet Plan, 151
Monoculture, 39, 96
Monopoly capitalism, 166
Morocco, 20
Motor tractor stations, 119

National Advisory Commission of Civil
        Disorders, 162
National defense
    expenditure, 152
    spending, 155
National Socialists, 131
Neoclassical economics, 10
Netherlands, 73
New Economic Policy (NEP), 117
New England, 73
New Guinea, 5
Nile, 4
Norman Conquest, 51
Nurkse, Ragnar, 34

Oligarchies, 75
Opium War, 140
Oppenheimer, Franz, 49
Overseer of the guild, 53
Owner-managers, 137

Pakistan, 20
Party of Revolutionary Institutions, 45
Patricians, 37, 41, 48
Pauperization, 26, 174
Payments before wages, 161
Pennsylvania, 46
Peonage, 45, 46
Peons, 38, 45, 46
Perpetual rents, 56
Phase, "take-off," 86
Phases and stages approach, 22, 23
Peripheral workers, 175
Philippines, 97, 98
Phoenicians, 73

Physiocrats, 58
Piecework compensations, 173
Pigou, A. C., 133
Plantation
    economy, 46
    system, 41
Plebeians, 48
Pockets of poverty, 154, 161
Poland, 46, 120
Polarization, 174
Polis, 47, 48
Postcolonialism, 59
Pre-Columbian
    America, 5
    empires, 165
Proletariat in rags, 175
Posthistorical phase of mankind, 26
Price control, 103
Priorities, 71
Producer cooperatives, 122
Production possibilities, 157
Productivity, 11
    trap, 33, 34
Profit
    after taxes, 170
    incentive system, 121
Promissory notes, 55
Protective tariffs, 90
Prussia, 140
Puerto Rico, 17, 83

Ranke, Leopold von, 22
Rationalization, economic, 137
Real income, protection of, 108
Recessions, 156
Recife, 97
Reconstruction assistance, 17, 135, 138
Redistribution of land, 95
Regional economic commissions, 19
Rent control, 131, 133
Revolution
    agricultural, 78, 92
    Bolshevik, 173
    Industrial, 35, 46, 56, 70, 78, 84,
        90, 92
Ricardo, David, 8
Rio de Janiero, 97
Rist, C., 168
Roepke, 133
Roman
    economic system, 5